the wrong ladder wondering what happened. Sonya makes the case for intentionally managing your career (like the work it takes to understand how promotions happen in companies) and teaches readers HOW to do the tough work we each must do: look inside to know ourselves first, set boundaries, know and communicate our values. For its clear step-by-step structure and the sprinkling of real stories of real people who Sonya has helped analyze their values and next steps, I will recommend this book to military service members and student veterans in transition who I serve at our nation's universities."

–**Graciela Tiscareño-Sato**, CEO Gracefully Global Group LLC, award-winning bilingual author/keynote speaker and facilitator of AUTHENTIC Personal Branding for Military Veterans workshops

"Most of us can look in hind sight and see a moment where we could have moved on more quickly from an unsatisfying job. Sonya's experiences and exercises help readers to more quickly identify and address those stuck moments. More importantly *WELCOME to the Next Level* invites people to take a step back and conduct a 360° review of what they value, how others value them, and the ways they might roadmap their path to greater career satisfaction."

–**Jill Finlayson**, Director of the Women in Tech Initiative at UC, Startup Consultant, and Advisor and Mentor to
T ᴸWomen

WELCOME to the Next Level

WELCOME
TO THE
NEXT LEVEL

3 Secrets to **Become Unstuck, Take Action,** *and* **Rise Higher** *in Your Career*

Sonya L. Sigler

NEW YORK

LONDON • NASHVILLE • MELBOURNE • VANCOUVER

WELCOME to the Next Level

3 Secrets to Become Unstuck, Take Action, and Rise Higher in Your Career

Published in New York, New York, by Morgan James Publishing in partnership with Difference Press. Morgan James is a trademark of Morgan James, LLC. www.MorganJamesPublishing.com

ISBN 9781642797633 paperback
ISBN 9781642797640 eBook
Library of Congress Control Number: 2019949503

Cover and Interior Design by:
Chris Treccani
www.3dogcreative.net

Morgan James is a proud partner of Habitat for Humanity Peninsula and Greater Williamsburg. Partners in building since 2006.

Get involved today! Visit
MorganJamesPublishing.com/giving-back

For my mom, Lee Sigler. This book would not be possible without you. Your support, in so many different ways, and encouragement mean everything to me. Thank you.

Table of Contents

Foreword

As founder and CEO of Thought Leadership Lab, I help leaders increase their influence, expand their impact, and leave a legacy that matters. Throughout my career, I've spent time mentoring and supporting other women and I am committed to cultivating women as leaders and executives. I started my career in the technology industry and founded my first company at age twenty-six, which started me down the path of becoming a serial entrepreneur.

Since then, I co-founded the Forum for Women Entrepreneurs (now Watermark) and the women's startup launch pad, Springboard Enterprises, which has since led to over $8 billion in funding for women entrepreneurs and their companies. I also co-founded Invent Your Future Enterprises and the Invent Your Future Conference for Women and I worked in politics for a short stint.

Although I'm proud of what I've accomplished, I will definitely admit that I've been stuck in my career many times and I've had to rethink and reboot my plan and my path over and over. I truly wish I'd had this book as a guide along the way. Instead, I had to learn to ask for help and advice and to reach out for support to lead my enterprises to success.

I first met Sonya in 1999 when I was running the Forum for Women Entrepreneurs and we implemented a mentor program using technology from a startup she was advising. From that point on, Sonya has joined me on my mission to help women entrepreneurs and leaders succeed – she as a consultant and advisor to startups and women founders, and me as a thought leadership consultant helping women build their visibility, credibility, and thought leadership to enhance their professional success.

Throughout her career as a lawyer and startup consultant, I have seen first-hand how Sonya has mentored women all along the way. Like me, she has rebooted and reimagined her career many times and she's learned many important lessons. I'm so glad that she's now written a book detailing her career journey and sharing her approach to mentoring and coaching. I know you're going to find it invaluable.

Whenever you find yourself stuck, at any point in your career, you'll want to read this book. Sonya walks you through her WELCOME to the Next Level process, which is a step-by-step guide to examine your goals and desires and to align them with your actions to rise higher in your career.

Sonya's Welcome Process starts with goal setting, which is much like peeling back the layers of an onion, to help you figure out what you want in your career. She then helps you envision your work-life mix and identify the gap between what you have now and where you want to go. The crux of the work is where she guides you through the process to know your own value and to be able to share that confidently with others inside your own company and beyond.

One thing I've learned from my own career is that you never know when you're going to face your next career crossroads. I've left jobs because I found myself out of alignment with the senior leadership team; I've been fired from roles that weren't a great fit; I've faced two major economic downturns that almost put my organizations out of business; and I've closed companies that I've started because customers just weren't clamoring for our products.

What I've learned is that success in your career is based on who you know and who knows you. When you're top of mind you get invited to take a seat at the table and when you're of service to others, you get invited back. Step 7 in Sonya's Welcome process – Externally Become Known – shows you exactly what to do to become better known – ideas I share with my clients at the Thought Leadership Lab.

If you are tired of being stuck or so frustrated you just want to quit your job, read this book for an immediate reframe and reset. Do the work Sonya outlines and you will make your own road map to take you higher in your career. You can't go wrong with her WELCOME to the Next Level Process as your guide and her as your mentor.

Denise Brosseau
Thought Leadership Lab, Founder & CEO
www.thoughtleadershiplab.com
Author of *Ready to Be a Thought Leader?: How to Increase Your Influence, Impact, and Success,*
Foreword by Guy Kawasaki
April 2019
Redwood Shores, CA

Introduction

I wrote this book as a guide for others to reach the next level in their career without having to go through what I went through. I want to share my knowledge and experience so that you can learn from the school of hard knocks and not have to make the same mistakes I did – that is, if they can even be called mistakes. Looking back, it seems more like naiveté or ignorance of how the real-world works.

My career has spanned a few different roles and responsibilities at companies of varying sizes – from brand-new startups to Fortune 500 companies. I started out as an in-house lawyer at a scrappy video game company. There I spent several years doing deals and learning the ropes with new products and new industries. After getting laid off, I went to a large financial services company and continued to make deals and negotiate agreements. From there I moved to consulting with startups and I considered myself a lawyer-turned-entrepreneur. A few years ago, I added coaching executives and senior leaders to my consulting business.

Throughout my career I have discovered that there are many ways to become stuck. Although what being stuck looks like may vary, the result is the same – failure to move forward or rise higher in your career. There are many lessons to be learned as a consequence.

What does being stuck look like? You are doing well in your career. In fact, you are getting the highest employee ratings in your annual review and receiving good feedback from those you work with. Yet you aren't being promoted. Why not?

You think that keeping your head down, working hard, and doing a good job will get you promoted. You think that doing a good job will be enough. It isn't.

Or you might not be getting the plum assignments that you used to. You start to wonder what is going on. What has changed? Slowly, without realizing it, you are no longer the "go-to" person.

You start seeing others get promoted and wonder, "How can that happen? How can Joe be getting a promotion. He doesn't do anything. He just talks a good game." It's so frustrating and aggravating when you see this happening around you. It's heartbreaking when others come up to you and ask, "Why weren't you promoted? You should be getting promoted instead of Joe!"

Then, you try to figure out what it actually takes to get promoted. You ask your boss for more information, yet you constantly get the runaround, or you get information that puts it off indefinitely. You might even be told, "Wait a few months and let's reevaluate where things are." Or worse, you get no actionable information as an answer.

You may be in a job that is just OK. You find yourself becoming bored. You've been in your position for a while and have done what you can do. You have a good boss and you like the company you work for, but you are getting more and more bored with your position. It's not bad enough to look for something else or actually leave the company. So you stay. But at what cost?

You may have even held several different positions for your company and been there for quite some time. Now what can you do? You've had so many roles, but it's been over such a long period of time, you can't even remember everything you have accomplished. You start to lose confidence that you can fit into the same role at another company because you are so entrenched in your current company.

You may have been at your company for so long that now you are taken for granted and no one has any idea what you are capable of doing. You are constantly frustrated trying to tell people that you can do things that you have done previously, but they are so new that they don't even know you have "been there, done that, and got the T-shirt."

Or you are sitting in your office in disbelief after having been chewed out by HR for doing something you thought was good, like winning an award or saving the company money by staying at a cheaper hotel rather than one on the approved travel list.

You may run into a political buzz saw, that is, someone who is actively trying to undermine you, either through harassment or bullying or through seemingly passive action, like forgetting to invite you to certain important decision-making meetings. You notice this only after it keeps happening a few times.

You may be working for a bad boss – someone who is uncertain in their own leadership capabilities or has low self-esteem even though they are the boss. They may be behaving in a way that is undermining, capricious, or unpredictable. They may just be a bad people person or a poor team manager.

You may find yourself becoming more and more frustrated at work to the point where you are angry. All the time. At first, you find yourself snapping at people for big things, then you find yourself snapping at the little things. When you snap at people for being human, you know you have a bigger issue to work through.

At first you take a sick day because you can't stand the thought of going in to the office. Before you know it, you are actually taking sick days because the stress has become too much and you just need a break. Or the stress has gotten so bad that it has manifested itself into a serious health problem or is causing you debilitating anxiety. Now you have a real health problem on your hands and actually need those sick days!

I have had to navigate my way through all kinds of scenarios like these. I learned the hard way to manage my own career path and not leave it in the hands of anyone else. I had to learn several times the importance of figuring out my own stories and sharing my own work experience. I had to learn to articulate what my top skills are clearly and quickly after being laid off unexpectedly. Despite all these setbacks, I figured out how to have a successful career.

I didn't let these obstacles stop me. I learned that it's not an impossible situation even though it may seem like it at the time. I learned that it is possible to overcome these setbacks.

Knowing how to manage your own career and articulate your stories and value to others will help you avoid the mistakes I made. I wrote this book to share what I have learned to help you rise higher and move to the next level of your career no matter what is causing you to be stuck.

Chapter 1:

The School of Hard Knocks

There Is No Way out but Through

"You must do the thing you think you cannot do."
– Eleanor Roosevelt

All I could think to myself was, "Is this all there is?"

I had wanted to be a lawyer forever, and I had worked hard to get where I was. I was an intellectual property lawyer at Sega, and I had been there a little over a year. This was my dream job. But after negotiating agreement after agreement, I thought, "This can't be all there is. Am I going to spend the next forty years doing this?" I figured out that I preferred making the deal to "papering" the deal as the lawyer.

In addition, I worked for a boss who many, including me, considered crazy. I figured out early on that I couldn't work for him and stay sane. I started to look for a new job even though I loved working at Sega.

In frustration one day, I mentioned potentially leaving the company to our vice president of product development, and he said, "I'd rather have you come work for me than leave the company." Yay! Problem solved. Not so fast. When we tried to make the change through HR and move me to making deals in the product development side, unbeknownst to me, my boss blocked it.

And then he made my life even more miserable. I started getting migraine headaches on Sunday afternoons, thinking about going back to work on Monday. This went on for months, it was debilitating and painful. I couldn't figure it out. I had never had any health problems before. Why these headaches?

Then there was news that we were being laid off. It was the fifth round of layoffs at Sega and even though we knew it would hit our department eventually, I didn't think it would hit me.

Ugh! Now what?

One of the services provided to laid-off employees was the opportunity to work with an outplacement agency. Now that sounds like fun, doesn't it? I was supposed to fill out this form detailing my work experience. I was supposed to use this information as the backbone of what would go into my résumé. They had a person available who would review your résumé and give you advice on making improvements and drafting cover letters. There was nothing offered that focused on identifying what my strengths were or teasing out my story.

I had my second interview for a contractor position at Intuit the day I got laid off at Sega. It was a time of recession, and I was happy to have another option. Not only did I not have to choose between a temporary contractor position over a full-time job, but I also postponed having to do any other job hunting and résumé work with the outplacement agency. This meant I didn't have to do any of that pesky work of figuring out what to put on my résumé or in any cover letters. I also didn't have to do any soul searching or self-reflection to figure out what I really wanted.

I started at Intuit two weeks later as a lawyer supporting several groups for both new and established products. After about eighteen months of contracting, I was hired as an employee with the title of corporate counsel.

Intuit was growing like gangbusters and was acquiring companies at a rate of about one per month. The due diligence process for each acquisition was intense, and I was quickly reaching the burnout stage. I had also just finished negotiating all of the agreements with banks all over the United States to download your banking data into Quicken with the push of a button. I was beginning to have that same thought I'd had at Sega: "Is this all there is?"

I had broached the subject with my boss about moving to another role within the company, doing business or corporate development, closer to the deal making source. She seemed supportive. Then we discovered we were both pregnant, with our babies due about three months apart.

About a month before her due date, my boss went home one day and went into labor with no transition or handoff to the person taking her place during maternity leave. In contrast, I was able to handpick the attorney who took my place during my leave.

Just prior to going out on maternity leave, I interviewed with one of our strategic partners. Their general counsel offered me a job on the spot to join the business affairs part of his team

– exactly what I had been trying to do at Intuit. Maybe it was the hormones or maybe it was the uncertainty of what I would want to do after I had my first child, but I took a few days to decide and ultimately turned down the offer.

When I thought about it, I really turned down the job out of a misplaced sense of loyalty to my boss and department, as well as the concern for the amount of work that I had on my plate and wanting a smooth product launch for both Quicken and Quicken Mortgage (which were products at Intuit). I learned the hard way that loyalty to a job and department doesn't pay.

I had been back at work for a couple of months after having my first child and was adjusting to fitting everything in. As I opened the door to our office building one morning, I remember thinking – "Wow! I don't hold my baby enough. I need to hold him more."

After that, I made a point to hold him as much as possible. He was only going to be a baby for a short period of time. It was a small epiphany and a small adjustment to make to make our lives better.

Unfortunately, at work, I didn't have that same epiphany or make that type of small adjustment. I stepped right back into the heads down, work hard mode I was used to before having a baby.

Shortly thereafter, I found out that my stand-in was being hired permanently – we were growing gangbusters by then, so I didn't think anything of it. Then, I found out he had quietly been promoted to a senior corporate counsel position.

You can imagine how upset I was. I had to learn the hard way that there was no way out but through. I went to my boss to have a conversation about what it takes to get promoted, understand why my stand-in was promoted, and so on. I got very few answers. In fact, I got no direction on what actually was required to be promoted.

It was pure folly to think that keeping my head down, working my butt off, and doing a good job would get me promoted. I thought that if I did a good job, that would be enough. In reality, I had no idea what my career path was.

It was then that I also realized that my boss (for whatever reason – feeling threatened or unsure of her own promotion) was not all that supportive of me – for a promotion or moving to another position within the company.

Until that point in time, I had avoided doing any work to be able to tell a clear story and to showcase my skills and strengths, especially as I was trying to move to the business side. I thought my work spoke for itself. Apparently, it did not.

I had to learn to be able to tell my own story, and in order to do so, I took advantage of the professional development classes at Intuit and learned to write my own vision and mission statement. The instructors had us do some soul searching and articulate our top five values and what was most important to us.

The moment I knew I was truly on my own was when we did the 360-degree feedback exercise. We had to gather feedback over the two weeks before we took this class. We were given a form for our boss, higher-ups, teams we worked with, and colleagues to fill out. I did this feedback gathering part diligently, and I brought it to the class with me.

When we came to that part of the exercise to read all the feedback and learn what others thought our top skills were, I opened the envelope eager to hear what others had to say about me. The one from my boss was blank. Blank. Not one word of feedback. What?!?

I felt the hot tears sting my face and run down my cheeks. The instructor hurried over to see what was going on and usher me out of the training – apparently, we couldn't continue without this essential piece of feedback.

My boss couldn't be bothered to give me feedback, let alone help me manage my career; something I had thought, mistakenly, bosses were supposed to do. It was then that I knew I had to manage my own career and share my work so that others knew about it.

The quote at the beginning of this chapter from Eleanor Roosevelt perfectly illustrates the position I found myself in – "You must do the thing you think you cannot do." This quote also applies to the work described in Chapter 7, "Own Your Value," because this storytelling work is the crux of what I learned the hard way. I had to be the one to tell my own story, even though it felt like bragging at first. I had to do the thing I thought I couldn't do – own my value, tell my story.

As I went out on my second maternity leave just a year after the first one, I figured out that I would need to leave the company to move to a higher level in my career. During that five-month maternity leave, I had an opportunity to hone my story and share it with startup CEOs. I left my in-house lawyer job to become the vice president of business development at IDO Systems, and finally I met my goal of moving to the business side of a company.

I loved working with startups over the next few years and being able to forge relationships and negotiate agreements from the business side, not just the legal side. We closed IDO Systems after two years of trying to make a go of it, and then I had my third child and a yearlong maternity "leave." I label it "leave" out of tradition, because I didn't have a job to go back to.

A friend of mine had joined a startup as general counsel, and she, knowing about my prior business development roles with startups, introduced me to the CEO. I had learned to tell my story and convey my value to CEOs by this time, and I was brought on as a founder and vice president of business development at Cataphora.

The CEO trusted me to take care of things for her and to make things happen, which I did for nine years through many leadership roles: vice president of business development, general counsel, CFO, vice president of client services, vice president of operations – basically anything that wasn't engineering. When we sold the company to Ernst & Young, I needed to find something else to do.

As I started to interview for general counsel and COO positions, I wasn't getting the warm and fuzzy response I had hoped for. Finally, one headhunter looked at my résumé and said frankly, "I don't know what to do with you. Do you want to be a general counsel or a COO?" The answer was yes, which didn't get me anywhere.

As I was wrapping up things at Cataphora, I had to clean out my office – which, if you are a pack rat archivist like me, will take you awhile! I started tossing things into the shredder bin, and I realized it had been so long that I had forgotten about certain projects or deals. I started keeping a list of what I had done and what I had achieved.

I realized that the things I had accomplished were far reaching and not at all what most general counsels do. I had to tell a better story about my experience. I had to narrow down my skills and superpowers to three to five things – not everything.

I worked hard over a couple month period to describe what I had done and could do in a way that resonated with CEOs. I was introduced to a CEO who didn't have an open general counsel or COO position but was intrigued enough with my experience to start a conversation. It took about six months of interviews and meetings to figure out how I could best help this company grow and change industries. I would put together a new consulting team focused on technology-assisted review and data analytics from several existing teams. Welcome to my new position as vice president of product strategy.

In doing this work, I hemmed and hawed and took months to identify my strengths and superpowers and to tell my own story. I was so used to advocating for others that I hadn't developed the skills to do that same thing for myself. It was so much easier to advocate for others.

I won't lie, the excavation work I needed to do to develop and learn to share my story wasn't easy. It took a lot of thought and reflection. It took my willingness to say what I wanted and equally as much, what I didn't want. For me, this process was like peeling back the layers of an onion. I learned a bit more each time I peeled back a layer and examined it. Doing the work for myself, I discovered a better way to figure out the building blocks that go into my story.

Through the work I did on my own storytelling journey, I developed the WELCOME to the Next Level Process. Now I spend my time teaching this process to others and working with individuals and companies, helping them become powerful storytellers – for themselves and for their teams and companies.

One client I helped through this exact process was Penny. She had recently changed from the insurance industry to fundraising and was in a relatively new position with a few notable wins under her belt. After our third session of working together, she had gained the confidence to ask for a promotion.

She called me excitedly to tell me that not only had she asked for a promotion and gotten it – she also received a new title and expanded role. Penny took ownership of her career and put it squarely into the hands of someone she could trust: herself. This is the exact same lesson I learned the hard way.

Now, I will lay out what the WELCOME Process is and how it can help you become unstuck, take action, and move to the next level in your career.

Chapter 2:

3 Secrets to Become Unstuck, Take Action, and Rise Higher in Your Career

The WELCOME to the Next Level Process — a Framework for Action

"A journey of a thousand miles begins with a single step."
– Chinese proverb

The WELCOME to the Next Level Process breaks down what I have learned on my journey to own my career path and manage my career. When I was so stuck and frustrated in my job, I moved my head above the trees so that I could see the forest. Once I could do that, I could see the path forward, and I didn't like where I was headed. I had to learn to trust my intuition and I had to figure out how to get clarity to be able to create the influence I wanted to have in my career.

All along, I was the key to my own success. I had to learn to advocate for myself. I had to stand up for myself and seek help. In doing this work, I discovered that all of this effort was not as hard or as bad as it first seemed. I took a hard look at those who were being promoted and who were flourishing in their careers, I drew a few conclusions, and these conclusions are the secrets to reaching the next level of your career.

The framework that I discovered to manage my own career boils down to these three secrets:

Secret 1: Goals Matter - Knowing yourself, what you want, and how you want to live your life is paramount to goal setting.
Having a goal will bring you clarity around what to pursue next and why. Establishing a goal will help you develop your own personal road map to follow for managing your career. This road map can be reviewed and changed at any time. But having a goal will give you direction.

Secret 2: Knowing Your Value Matters – With or without your consent or cultivation, your personal brand is the story told to attract people to you.
Knowing your strengths will allow you to articulate what value you bring to the table. Once you know your unique strengths and superpowers, you will be able to develop stories to convey your value to others.

Secret 3: Sharing Your Value Matters – Get over your reluctance to be known and take personal responsibility for what others know about you, inside and outside of your company.
Sharing your value with others in your company will make your work known to those who have the power to promote you. Sharing your value with others externally in your industry will

make you and your work known to others rather than leaving you or it to languish in obscurity. These connections and relationships within your company and outside your company are the ones you will need to cultivate to find your next position.

These secrets are essential to manage your own career and they are deceptively simple. To move to the next level, I needed to examine and explore what each secret meant to me and my career path. As I did this work, I developed the WELCOME to the Next Level Process to break down each secret into bite-sized chunks of work. I refer to it as the WELCOME Process and I am sharing it with you so that you do not have to reinvent the wheel. You can benefit from this solution and get the help you need to make a change and move your own career forward.

The WELCOME Process is designed to help you take action in your career at any time, immediately today or in the future. Here's a summary of each step of the WELCOME Process:

Step 1: <u>W</u>ho Are You?
Peel back the layers of your fundamental beliefs and values to identify what is most important to you. Identifying these nonnegotiable items is essential to designing your own career road map.

Step 2: <u>E</u>nvision Your Work-Life Mix
Look at your entire life picture – the mix or balance of what you want at work and what you want in your home life, as the two are inextricably intertwined.

Step 3: <u>L</u>ocate the Gaps

Find the gap between what you want and what you have. This will give you guidance on what to change and what to do next. The bigger the gap, the more frustrated and stuck you will be in your job. The smaller the gap, the happier and more satisfied you will be with your career.

Step 4: Call Out Your Strengths

Define your strengths and skills to make it easier to articulate what you offer to others and position yourself in other's minds how you want to be seen and perceived.

Step 5: Own Your Value

Develop authentic and memorable stories that explain or showcase your experience. This will make it easier for you to share your value with others. Owning your achievements and stories gives you the confidence to share these stories with others.

Step 6: Make Yourself Known Internally

Share your work and your stories internally at your own workplace as that will make your work more widely known and appreciated. Being known by others is the key to get promoted at any job, especially your next job.

Step 7: Externally Become Known

Share your work and stories externally beyond your company, throughout your industry, and beyond. This will get you noticed in a broader network. Should you decide to leave your job, you will have already cultivated a network to help you move to the next level.

What You'll Find in Each Chapter

Each chapter of the WELCOME Process is structured to include a quote, tips and advice, exercises, relatable stories, the expected result, and how it may apply to a team or company in a way that is different than for individuals.

The quotes for each chapter are intended to inspire you and capture the essence of the chapter message. The tips and advice are what I have found to work for me and for my clients.

I explain the exercises that you will need to do to become unstuck, take action, and move forward in your career. Each step includes one exercise, and in some cases, more than one exercise to help you uncover essential information to use for your transformation.

I have included my own stories and many client stories to illustrate how any situation where you are stuck or frustrated can be changed even though it doesn't feel like it at the time. All client names have been changed. These stories are also included to share with you that many others are in the same position as you: facing the same frustration and stuck-ness and trying to figure out what to do about it.

Each step also details the expected results if you do the included exercises. The results achieved with the work in each step depends on you and the effort you put in. For each exercise, there is a direct correlation: The more effort you put in, the more effective your results will be.

The steps and the exercises not only apply to individuals who are stuck or frustrated in their career, but the WELCOME Process also applies to stuck or dysfunctional teams and companies. If your team or company is having employee retention and employee satisfaction issues, then doing this work at the team or company level can peel back the onion layers on what is really happening. Leaders of teams or companies can do this exact same work at the team or company level to rebuild and make changes. To the extent that the work is different for a team or company, I will explain more at that point in the chapter. Otherwise, the work is the same for a team or a company wishing to make changes.

The Work and What It Means

The work described in the WELCOME Process can be done at any time. You can use the work for a particular step as a reference or checkpoint in your career. For example, if you find that your stories aren't resonating with others any longer, you may want to reread Chapter 7 on owning your value to work on refining your stories. Or if you want to become more widely known in your company, you can do the work in Chapter 8. The work for any of the WELCOME steps can be done as a checkpoint at any time in your career.

Mind-mapping is a technique that I find very helpful to use with the work and exercises described throughout the book. The technique is simple – you write down the one goal in the middle and circle it. Then you draw a line to the next detail to meet that goal and then repeat it for as many details as you can think of.

The map you have drawn can help clarify your thinking around that goal. I have included a mind map example:

This mind-mapping technique can be used at any time you become stuck or start spinning your wheels about an issue. If you don't know where to start, try using the mind-mapping technique to write down all of your thoughts about your situation. Mind-mapping may be mentioned for particular steps where it is an effective method to help you clarify your thoughts. You can do mind-mapping with a pen and piece of paper, or there is even an app for it.

Keeping a journal as you do the work in this book is very helpful. Some of the work, although simple, requires you to reflect on the underlying reasons for your situation and the why behind your beliefs. Tracking your thoughts and observations in a journal can help you move forward more quickly. Gathering your thoughts and feelings together and writing about them can be cathartic as well, especially when you are frustrated in your current job. Writing about this situation will help you identify exactly why you are frustrated and will help to illuminate what you need to do to make a change.

At the end of each chapter there will be a "More Resources" section. This section will list any book or study mentioned in that chapter as well as other helpful resources. It will also list the exercises mentioned in that chapter and will point you to the place on my website where you can get a blank exercise worksheet to use anytime with any WELCOME Process step.

It's time to reach the next level of your career!

Secret 1: Goals Matter

The first secret to reaching the next level of your career is that goals matter. Knowing yourself, what you want, and how you want to live your life is paramount to goal setting. Whether it's reaching a certain position – senior director, vice president, general counsel, or CEO – or having the flexibility to live your desired lifestyle, having a goal will keep you motivated to do the work and to reach the next level.

I wanted to be a lawyer since I was fourteen. I had an amazing US history teacher, Mrs. Grinkmeyer, who taught us the US Constitution and how important it was to our democracy. I thought it was an amazingly elegant document, and I wanted to become a lawyer, with the lofty goal of upholding our Constitution. I was 100 percent committed to this goal. For the next eleven years, my goal of becoming a lawyer governed every decision I made.

The good news is that I became a lawyer at 25. The bad news is that when I had been a lawyer at Sega for a little over a year, I thought to myself, "Is this all there is? I'm going to negotiate agreement after agreement after agreement? For the next 40 years?" Wow. That does not sound appealing at all. Crap. Now what?

I had to figure out what my next goal was because the thought of negotiating agreement after agreement bored me to tears. I really loved the art of the negotiation and making the deal, I just didn't love papering it. I wanted to get to the business side, not just stay on the legal side of the business.

Check. I had a new goal. I had clarity. I had direction: get to the business side.

The next three chapters break down what goes into setting your own goals as they relate to your work and life.

- Chapter 3 covers Step 1 of the WELCOME Process – Who Are You? I will discuss knowing yourself and your values and why self-exploration is important.
- Chapter 4 covers Step 2 of the WELCOME Process – Envision Your Work-Life Mix. You will explore how you want to live your life, what you envision in your work and life, and what the mix of the two should be.
- Chapter 5 covers Step 3 of the WELCOME Process – Locate the Gaps. I will instruct you on how to do a gap analysis to locate the gap between where you are and where you want to be and explore what that means in terms of action.

These three chapters detail the work required to have a goal, which is the first secret to reaching the next level of your career.

Chapter 3:

<u>W</u>ho Are You?

Know Yourself and What You Want

"If you don't know where you are going,
any road will get you there."
– Lewis Carroll, *Alice in Wonderland*

The first step of the WELCOME Process is to look at who you are and figure out what you want. Knowing yourself and articulating your top values is the foundation of the work in this step. As part of this exploration, look deeper into how you like to spend your time and how you do not like to spend your time. Knowing yourself includes putting together a list of "must haves" as well as "cannot haves." Finally, you'll examine what energizes you and what drains your energy.

The most important idea to understand when setting and reaching your goals is to know who you are and what you want. I hear from so many people, "I don't know what I want." When I had a hard time finding my next job, the crux of the problem was not knowing what I wanted. It is hard to find your dream job or figure out what is next if you don't know what you want.

Others have a hard time helping you if you cannot clearly articulate to them what you want. They are left knowing you need help and wanting to help you, but they have no idea or clarity around who or what kind of job to refer you to. As the quote from Lewis Carroll at the beginning of this chapter states, "If you don't know where you are going, any road will get you there." Without a clear goal, you can't figure how to get there, nor can anyone else.

The first part of getting clear and figuring out what you want is knowing who you are. Some people have a clear idea of who they are. I am a creative advocate, and it took me a long time to put those two words together. I was always fighting for others and for what is right. As a freshman in high school, I rallied a group of unhappy band members together to go see the school principal to get our band director fired. Who does that at fourteen? An advocate.

Realizing that being creative was an essential ingredient of who I am gave me additional clarity. Just because I am an advocate doesn't necessarily mean I will like being a lawyer, as I discovered the hard way. I learned early in my career that I needed an element of creativity in my work.

The licensing work was too repetitive to satisfy me on a daily basis; I needed to learn, do research, figure out how things worked, and then invent a new way of doing things. I gravitated to this new work, the innovative side of the company, the new business development team. To stay engaged, I needed the creative aspect and the advocacy component.

Your career happiness and satisfaction depend on the alignment between (1) who you are and what you value and (2) what your actions are at work (and home). If you already have clarity around knowing who you are and what you want, you can read this chapter as a refresher for refinement. But if you don't know what you value most or you can't articulate what you want, you'll need to dig a little deeper to figure this out so you can become unstuck.

Knowing who you are breaks down into what you value, how you like spending your time, and figuring out what your bottom-line requirements are and what energizes you. Let's look at each of these in more detail.

Your Values

What do you value the most? What is important to you? This part takes a little reflection, some introspection, and a lot of awareness to figure out. Look all the way back to childhood to what you wanted to be when you grew up. Are you doing that now? Why or why not? Also take a look at statements that begin with "I wish": "I wish I could do ____." These kinds of statements are revealing of your true desires.

Well, I told you a bit about my story of wanting to be a lawyer since I was in the eighth grade. There was another part to that story: I also wanted to be the first female president and the first female principal trombonist of the Berlin Philharmonic. Might as well start at the top!

I did go into politics and I have run for office many times. I was on the school board for fourteen years. But at the end of the day, I discovered that I really hate the BS and posturing in politics. I am much more real than that. With that realization, my goal of being president went out the window.

My career as a trombonist is still going, albeit not in the Berlin Philharmonic. There aren't that many professional trombone positions that come open. I was lucky enough to audition for the second trombone position in the San Francisco Symphony when I was eighteen. At the same time, I was deeply into earning my undergraduate degree as fast as possible to get to law school. If I had been offered the position, I would have had a very interesting, possibly difficult, choice of choosing between being a musician or a lawyer. It was a false choice because you can be both, but there will be trade-offs. My point with these two examples is that I had strong goals from childhood, and I pursued them even though they didn't work out as I had hoped or imagined.

The last part I want to share about childhood goals – what I want to be when I grow up – is that some people have these understandings about themselves and they pursue that relentlessly. Others never have this type of clarity. For insight into what you value, look back to see what excited you and what you loved to do as a child.

I used to love to play "school." One of the things I do and have done my entire career is teach and share my knowledge and what I have learned. I have examples from almost every aspect of my life where I have done this – from on the job mentoring to teaching high school classes to giving webinars, on subjects including yoga, music, statistics, business, and law, to ages ranging from kindergartners to adult professionals.

If you look back to what you wanted to be when you grew up and start to look for more of that throughout your life, you will begin to see a pattern of what you love. If your career is aligned with this love, you will experience happiness and satisfaction with your job. If there is no alignment between your job and what you love, you may be unhappy, you may want to quit your job on the spot most days, or you may end up burned out and stuck.

One of the exercises I work through with clients is a "Who Are You" questionnaire. It contains questions that get to the essence of who you are and what you value. One client answered these questions and rediscovered that she loved connecting to people and selling things. She used to love to set up lemonade stands and hold yard sales, and she had always been a top seller of Girl Scout cookies in her troop. She noticed that she wasn't using her people connection and sales skills in her current career. She changed over to a sales role and prospered in it. It was a match for who she was and what she loved to do. Her happiness and contentment with her career blossomed.

When there is alignment with what is important to you and your values, there is an ease and simplicity to your life. Figuring out what is important to you can give you the clarity you need to make more aligned choices.

Last spring, my oldest son was sitting in an airport waiting for a delayed flight. He took the time to write down everything that was important to him, what he valued. Besides this being a super-proud-mommy moment for me, I told him I was impressed that he did this at twenty, in his second year of college. Most people never write a list like this in their entire life.

My list is short – I want to be doing work that makes a difference. That's why I wrote this book. That's why I volunteer for various groups, fundraise, and mentor women. I have a high level of intellectual curiosity and it is the trait I most value in my partner and those closest to me. I value education and lifelong learning, so it is no surprise that I teach others at all levels. I value fairness, equality, and justice, so it is no surprise that I am a lawyer and work to empower women. Or that I can't stand situations that are not fair. Countless times I have uttered, "That's not fair!" and then worked to change things, make them better, fairer.

To put together a list of your top five or even top ten values won't take long. If you are having trouble thinking of the words to articulate your values, you can do a couple of things: First, think about a time when you were mad or upset with someone or a situation. The value that is being violated will be revealed in that scenario. Second, you can take a look at the end of the chapter under "More Resources" for a link to a list of values or you can do a quick search on the internet for values, and you will find long lists of words that are values you might hold. Assembling your list is the beginning step of designing your own life and career, setting goals that are aligned with what you really want, and transitioning from a life of "should" to a life of "Yes, I want to do this."

When you start putting your list of values together, you will start to notice little incongruences between that list and what is happening in your life at home and work. I value my freedom to choose what I am going to do each day and I hate to be micromanaged or told what to do. I try to avoid working with micromanagers if at all possible – and this includes any volunteer work. I also value integrity. I worked at one company where people would say something in a meeting and then do the opposite after walking out of the meeting. After about a year at that job, I started getting migraines on Sunday afternoons. It was a physical manifestation of the mismatch in integrity levels between what I valued and the company I was working for.

As you put together your list of top values, start to notice where there is alignment and where there are incongruences in your life. Only then can you start to make changes to bring your life in alignment with what it is you want.

How You Spend Your Time

Another way to figure out who you are and what matters to you is to look at how you like or, more importantly, don't like spending your time – at work and at home. One of the exercises I work through with clients is how they spend time and what their work style is.

I have a ton of hobbies – sewing, knitting, scrapbooking, photography, auto-crossing Porsches, cooking with my husband for our friends and family, hiking and visiting national parks (after all, my three boys are named after national parks), playing trombone, singing and dancing in community theater, and traveling and exploring the world. Through all these experiences, I discovered that I love to work on a project at a balls-to-the-wall level for a few weeks or months and then take a break.

Looking back, I would have been a better student in college with quarters rather than semesters because that sustained effort and time frame was too long for me. It is the same with theater productions. You work at high intensity for a short amount of time and then take a break and work at a lower level of effort before starting the cycle again. That intensity level and time frame is a better match for me.

This realization would have really mattered to me when I was so burned out at Intuit, doing acquisition after acquisition. There was no real break in there to regroup and reset because the deals were continuous and overlapping. Had I known this about myself at the time, I might have been able to approach my workload differently.

Understanding how you don't want to spend your time is just as important to knowing yourself. In fact, it may be more important to helping you figure out who you are and what you want or don't want. I want my work and contribution to be appreciated. I worked on a couple of projects where I felt like my contributions were not valued. I now end those projects or situations as soon as possible.

Also look at how you do not want to be spending your time. I worked for one boss who would manufacture a crisis on Fridays at 4:00 p.m., give or take an hour. This was at a time when most tech companies would have happy hour and people would be hanging out talking about work or their weekend plans. It was definitely not a time for starting new projects.

This boss would come up with some whopper of a project that had to be done over the weekend. After two or three times of this happening, I realized he never, and I mean NEVER, even looked at the work I had done on these "crisis" projects.

So, I stopped being available on weekends for those kinds of projects. I would work on the weekend if, in my judgment, my business unit clients needed the work completed prior to Monday morning. I never again worked on the weekends for one of his projects. He was the general counsel, and it was a career limiting move, for sure, but I wasn't going to work on something that wasn't even looked at. That is a blatant example of doing work that wasn't appreciated, and it was in direct conflict with one of my core values.

One of my clients, Abby, works at a company with many government contracts, and there can occasionally be time in between projects where she is looking for interesting or challenging work with another project or team. During these times, backlogged or unessential work is assigned, and she was tasked with logging documents from the 1960s for archival project. After we worked together, you can bet she did everything she could to be assigned to more meaningful and appreciated work.

Requirements Road Map

When I work with clients on how they want to spend their time, I also have them work through a "requirements" road map exercise for their job – what is essential, what is nice to have, and what are deal breakers. Sometimes we expand the scope of this exercise to include their entire life, especially if they are really stuck or in a state of being overwhelmed. But we'll explore that mix in more depth in the next chapter. I usually ask that they take about twenty minutes to list ten things for each category. Below is a sample road map from my client Belinda, who was trying to figure out if she could reframe her current position or if she needed to quit her job and move on.

Sample Requirements Road Map

Must Have

1. Salary commensurate with current income $130,000+
2. Contributed Retirement Plan
3. Good Health Plan: Medical, Dental & Vision
4. Team-oriented environment
5. Managerial/operational position

Nice to Have

1. Proximity to home or flexible hours or work-from-home options
2. Supportive work environment
3. Possibility to work on business processes
4. Training staff, lead team motivation
5. Some travel OK
6. Financial planning and budgeting responsibilities
7. Income that will allow saving money
8. Bonus structure that measures accomplishments
9. An inspiring position
10. Mid-size company with stability

Cannot Have

1. Dictator boss
2. Noncollaborative environment
3. Salary that does not support expenses
4. Commission-based income
5. A boring position

Once you are done making your initial list, review it to check if anything is missing. Check for any inconsistencies among the three lists. If so, rework the lists so that there are no inconsistencies. Over the next week or so, you will be thinking about this list over and over. When you see particular behavior at your current job or situation, it will trigger something that belongs somewhere on this list. Add to it, edit it. It's your list. The clearer you are in developing your requirements list, the easier it is to find a job or career that fits your requirements.

What Energizes You

If you look at your day-to-day tasks, you will quickly be able to see which ones give you energy and which ones drain you of energy. When I give a talk or workshop, seeing the aha moments in others energizes me. As a coach, seeing the transformation in my clients energizes me. But when I sit down to do follow up or start writing an email, I get fidgety, or I get up to make or grab a snack. The laundry looks good. You get the picture – that work does not energize me. In fact, it takes so much energy to start those tasks that I often just avoid them for as long as possible.

I remember clearly in the third grade when I was chosen as the class ambassador. It was an honor to be selected and my role as the ambassador was to show the new kids around, help them acclimate to a new environment, and teach them the ropes. I loved it. When I look back at what I have done in my career and life, I can clearly see what was energizing – the challenging work, teaching others, relationship building, the marshalling together of people to put on a show, to solve a problem, or to invent some new process or procedure to make things work better. All of that energized me.

I can also see what saps my energy and eliminates all motivation – doing work that isn't appreciated, routine tasks, working with jerks or people I don't trust, working within a broken process or procedure, or most marketing- and sales-related tasks. All of these activities drain my energy and make me want to avoid them like the plague.

At one company, I was running the entire administrative side and I had set up the systems for accounts payable and receivable and the database to gather time tracking information for billing purposes – that was all great – it was exciting and challenging to set up the systems to meet our needs. But when it started to become routine about six months in, I dreaded doing the repetitive tasks. The CEO and I had a conversation that went like this:

> **CEO:** You have done all this work to set up the systems and send our invoices out and bring in money to the company on a timely basis.
> **Sonya:** It's been working great.
> **CEO:** But this work is making you miserable.
> **Sonya:** Yes. Yes, it is.
> **CEO:** Let's find something else for you to spend your time on.

We ended up hiring a controller and a new CFO and moving me over to concentrate on building out our operations and client services functions. This example shows clearly that others will definitely notice that certain work or tasks sap your energy.

When my clients find themselves stuck and drained of energy at work, I have them do this Energize Me exercise. For a week, keep a daily log of what activities you are doing at work and at home. Note whether each one energizes you (+), drains you of energy (–), or is neutral (=). After a week of doing this, it will be clear which activities sap your energy and which ones energize you.

Through the work in this chapter, you can discover more about who you are, what you value, and whether your activities give you or sap your energy. Your level of career happiness and satisfaction depend on the alignment between knowing who you are, what you want and what you are actually doing with your time. The closer the alignment, the higher the level of satisfaction and happiness. The bigger the gap in alignment, the higher your frustration and feeling of stuck-ness levels will be.

How aligned is what you want with what you are doing?

When doing this work at the team or company level, the work in this chapter must be done on an individual level and team or company level in order to align the team values with those of the individual team members. The same exercises can be applied to a team. For example, a sales team will have its own goals and values for the team. Knowing who the team is and what the team mission is can help the individuals assess whether they are a fit. The same goes for company-level goals and values.

In summary, Step 1 of the WELCOME Process is to figure out who you are, which includes knowing yourself and what your top values are, how you like and dislike spending your time, what your bottom-line requirements are, and knowing what energizes you. Now that you have a good idea of who you are and what matters to you most, you can envision what you want in your work-life mix, which is the next step in the WELCOME Process.

More Resources

Books:
Designing Your Life: How to Build a Well-Lived, Joyful Life by Bill Burnett & Dave Evans
https://amzn.to/2U2xzSO

Exercises:
- Who Are You – A set of questions designed to dig deeper into who you are.
- Values – What are your top three to five values?
- Time – How do you like to spend your time? What is your preferred work style?
- Requirements Road Map – What is your bottom-line set of requirements?
- Energize Me – What energizes you? What drains you?

These exercises are available at
www.sonyasigler.com/book_bonuses

A Goal-Setting Workshop is available on request at
www.sonyasigler.com/workshops

Chapter 4:

Envision Your Work-Life Mix

What Is Your Work-Life Vision?

*"It's better to be at the bottom of the ladder you want
to climb than the top of one you don't."*
– Stephen Kellogg, musician.

Step 2 in the WELCOME process is to envision your work-life mix. Take a look at what you want for your work life and your personal life for the short- and long-term, as well as your lifetime goals. You'll explore what that looks like in a vision board. Visions can change and your work-life mix can get out of whack with what you truly desire. When that happens, you need to reassess your work-life mix and make adjustments.

I use the word mix specifically because I believe work-life balance doesn't exist and is fundamentally an unattainable goal. It's an impossible dream that we, mostly as women, have been sold. What is possible is that you define what mix of work and life commitments you want to make and what boundaries you want to set around each part of your life.

When I was changing jobs and getting divorced (by the way – I don't recommend making these two monumental changes at the same time), I took the opportunity to say to myself, "What do I want in my personal life?" and "What do I want in my work life?" I had the mindset of "Now that I can really start over and build my life in a way that I want, what can it look like?" I took the time to work through the exercises in the prior chapter and to think through what I wanted most for the next few years.

Once I realized that my career satisfaction rested on knowing what I wanted for work and for life, then I had to figure out exactly what that mix looked like. That work-life vision is what I will explain in this chapter.

Work-Life Vision: Short-Term and Long-Term Goals

I use a Work-Life Vision exercise with clients to help them figure out and define what they want their work-life mix to be.

What is your vision for your work life? Do you want to travel? Do you like to be in an office setting? Do you want to be around people, or do you prefer to work remotely? Are you bored with your work? Do you want more of a challenge? Do you want a job that you can leave behind every day when you leave the office?

What is your vision for your personal life, at home? Do you have a spouse or children? Is your spouse away from home and traveling a lot? Are your children out of the house or are you beholden to a school schedule? Do you have hobbies that take up a certain amount of time or space? Golf is a long game compared to tennis. Woodworking requires a lot of equipment.

Can your hobbies be integrated into other parts of your life? I read when I travel, and I'm known for knitting during meetings.

These questions are just the tip of the iceberg when it comes to what you envision for yourself for your work-life mix. One of the questions I often ask clients is, "What do you want to be doing that you currently don't have time for?" The answer to this question usually leads to something they want to put on their work-life vision list.

When I was laid off at one company, I had to figure out what to do next. As that position had been custom made for me, what I found next would definitely not look like that same job. I started looking for a full-time position, and in the meantime, I started consulting. As I continued down the path of consulting and looking for a full-time position, I recognized that more than anything else, I wanted to control my own schedule.

Looking forward to the next few years, I realized all my boys were in high school or would be shortly and that I wanted to be able to see them play sports and be available to them while they were still at home. As one of their team photographers, I wanted to be on the sideline for their football games and baseball games (but wrestling, not so much!) That meant being available Friday afternoons and evenings during the fall for football and in the afternoons two days a week during the spring for baseball games. The reality of commuting to another job an hour away would make it impossible to attend their games. I chose to keep consulting and work at home so I could be there for my boys.

One client, Christine, was feeling so overwhelmed she came to me in a state of pure desperation to help her out of the chaos her life had become. We took a look at all of her commitments between her role as CEO of her own company and her commitments as a wife and as a mother of three children. We worked through the Work-Life Vision exercise.

First, we looked at the reality of her situation with three kids in three different schools and what that meant for her morning and afternoon routines. Then we added the reality of their family having one car and her role of taking her husband to the train station every morning. We added in the nonnegotiable items from the Requirements Road Map in the prior chapter, which included Zumba or other physical activities to get a more complete work-life picture for Christine. All of these nonnegotiable items left about five to six hours a day for her to run her global business. This reality changed her mind-set and expectations of what she could get done with her current commitments for both work and her personal life.

If you had asked me what my work-life vision was when my kids were younger, I would have said, "The inside of my eyelids." Wait, what? What kind of a vision is that? I was so exhausted and burned out from raising three kids, volunteering, being on the school board, having a more than full-time job at a startup that required travel, and so on, I would have said my vision is to sleep. Get some rest. Heck, I just wanted to feel rested. I was tired of being tired.

If I had stepped back for a moment to reflect on what I really wanted, I might have come up with a different mix of what I wanted between work and my home life. If I'd only had a vision instead of just jumping on the relentless hamster wheel of work, kids, sports, laundry, I might not have crashed into the waves of a divorce and job change at the same time.

This Work-Life Vision exercise helps you answer the following questions: What do you want your work life to be like? What do you want your home life to be like? There are no right or wrong answers here. It's up to you. You make it what you want. You design your unique mix of work and life. What works for your colleague may not work for you.

The mind map for my current Work-Life Vision:

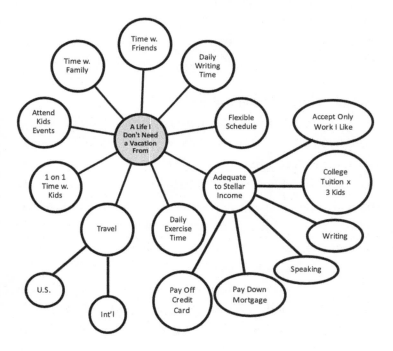

One note of reality – you can't do everything at the same time. The pieces of your home and work lives fit together like a puzzle. There is a natural ebb and flow to life. What worked when you were single, like picking up and traveling to Europe on a whim, may not work for you when you have three kids in school, and you are the one who drives them.

Setting a vision for your work and personal lives will bring you clarity and help you to set the next logical goal for each part. Having these goals defined will narrow the path you are on. You can easily minimize distractions by sticking to your plan. Setting this vision for yourself makes it easy for you to say yes to things that align with your vision and no to the things that don't. Having this vision and your reason why you do what you do will keep you from becoming overwhelmed and will keep you on track for making your vision a reality.

Bucket List: Your Lifetime Goals List

I highly recommend keeping a bucket list, which is a list of things you want to do or achieve in your lifetime, before you "kick the bucket." There's even the movie The Bucket List that you might check out for fun. I keep a running bucket list and try to do a few items on it each year. Recently, I have taken belly dancing lessons and lived in Singapore for a month. Next up is ballroom dancing lessons with my husband, which is actually an item from our joint bucket list.

There is an often-cited, albeit fictional, study done at Harvard in 1979 about the importance of goal setting. A group (3 percent) wrote down a list of goals plus an action plan. A second group (13 percent) wrote down goals only. Another group (84 percent) did not write down any goals. The researchers followed this group for 10 years and discovered that the group of 3 percent who had written goals and an action plan had out earned the other 97 percent by ten times.

A similar study was actually conducted by psychology professor Gail Matthews in 2007 at the Dominican University of California (not Harvard 1979 or Yale 1953, as every other claim cites, even by greats such as Zig Ziglar and Tony Robbins), and she found evidence for the effectiveness of writing down one's goals as well as the power of accountability in sharing your goals with a friend. From Matthews' report: "This study provides empirical evidence for the effectiveness of three coaching tools: accountability, commitment, and writing down one's goals."

It may seem simple to make a bucket list, but it is an important part of making a vision for yourself and achieving that vision. If you want to travel to France, put that on your bucket list. If you want to explore auto-crossing, put that on your bucket list. If you want to make vice president by the time you are thirty, put it on your list. Nothing is too big or too small to go on your list. I have one silly item on my list from a time in junior high school way back in 1979 – having Bo Derek braids (the real name is Fulani braids with beads or cornrows). One day, I'll go on a tropical vacation to some island and have these braids done to my very long, straight hair and pretend to look like Bo Derek as she walks on the beach in the movie 10.

Naming it and listing your goal is the first step to achieving it. Here is a sample from my current bucket list:

[ ] Own and live in a house on a lake – the Love Shack!

[ ] Bartender license, ABC certification

[ ] Hike Pacific Coast Trail

[x] Take a water color class

[x] Take a drawing class

[ ] Roller derby

[ ] Bicycle built for two – try in LA over New Years

[ ] Sundance Film Festival

[ ] Sun Valley Idaho

[ ] Zip lining

[ ] Bungee Jumping

[ ] Helicopter ride

[ ] Skydiving

[ ] Visit every National Park

[ ] Visit every state (North Dakota, Montana, Alaska left)

[ ] Billy Joel in concert – meet him

[ ] Elton John in concert – meet him

[ ] Adele concert

[x] Beach Blanket Babylon

[ ] Northern Lights in Scandinavia or Alaska

[ ] Safari in Africa

[ ] Galapagos

[ ] Machu Picchu

[ ] Drive Mercedes Gullwing on the track at Laguna Seca

[ ] Own one from 1950s

[ ] Bo Derek braids

It's important to take your list out and review it, adjust it, and cross off items on it. Take action. Don't just stick it in a drawer and never look at it again. Take action – yes, I know I said this part just a moment ago, but it is important enough to repeat. I try to do one or two things on my bucket list every year. This past year, we went to see Beach Blanket Babylon, and I took drawing and water color classes. Better yet, I try to combine them if possible – we will be taking a helicopter ride in Alaska as we chase the Northern Lights this year. As I hear myself saying, "Oh, I'd like to try that." So, I whip out my phone, open Evernote and add it to my note called, simply enough, "Bucket List."

Vision Boards

One tangible way to envision your work-life mix is to make a vision board with images and words depicting what you want. I hadn't done a vision board in many years until recently, after talking to our vice president of sales in his office where he had a huge vision board hanging from the ceiling. You couldn't miss it – it would hit you in the head if you didn't duck when coming into his office. I asked him about it and he explained several of the pictures on the two-sided vision board. Two things stuck with me – the giant wad of one hundred-dollar bills smack in the middle of his vision board and the picture of this exquisitely happy couple walking arm in arm. He explained that he wanted to stay at the top of his game as a sales person and make extraordinary money. He also explained that he and his wife wanted to have a baby and remain the happy couple they are now.

I promptly went home and made my own vision board (did I mention the simultaneous job change and divorce?). I put together images and words that depicted what I had envisioned for work and my personal life. I have been making vision boards each year since and my new husband has even joined me in making a joint vision board for what we want in our married life.

Putting together a vision board is simple if you have clarity around what you want. The work you have done so far in figuring out who you are and what you want feeds right into this exercise to make your own vision board. Vision boards can be created for different purposes. I created one for my business and what I want to achieve in my business. I even created one when I worked with a coach when I was getting divorced. That one had a lot of barbed wire on it – yikes. I have made vision boards with my husband for what we want in a honeymoon and another one for our house. I have made these for theater shows I have produced. Whatever you want to envision you can bring it to life visually by making a vision board – physically or virtually.

When you are ready to create your own vision board, gather magazines, scissors, a poster board, and a glue stick (and if you like a little sparkle in your life, a few glitter glue pens). Take a look at the magazines and cut out words or images that resonate with what you want in your work-life vision. Play around with the placement of the words and images on the poster board until you find a placement that suits you and your vision. Glue everything down, use the glitter glue pens if you want, or not! Once the boards are complete, you can laminate them so they will last longer. Snap a picture and email it to me at info@ sonyasigler.com.

Hang your vision board in a place where you will see it. I hung the one I created, after my chat with our top sales guy, in my office at work. When I created one for the next year, I hung the prior one on the back of my bedroom door so I would see it every morning and evening. Now they have a place on the inside of my closet door as well.

In the vision board workshops I hold, I have seen all kinds of vision boards created – from words only to nine pictures (think Instagram), to a "made-to-order" type list, to the usual images and words combined in a hodge-podge mix. It all works. There is no right way or wrong way to create a vision board. It works because your vision board is made to suit your vision and what you want.

Continuous Process: Adjust Your Vision

The process of envisioning what you want in your work life and personal life is not a one-and-done situation. Life is not static. Things change, life happens. You can choose to change paths deliberately or you can evaluate opportunities as they arise. Whichever way you do it, it is important to evaluate periodically what your vision is and how you are doing. Sometimes you get stuck in a rut and you can't figure out what to do next. Reevaluate your work-life vision and figure out if you need to adjust it or make changes.

One of the things I had in mind to do after I was done working with startups was working in the national parks. I love being outdoors, hiking, camping, exploring – all that. I thought becoming a national park ranger or even a park docent giving tours would be a fabulous way to explore the parks when I "retired."

The place where we camp every summer, the Lair of the Bear, had an opening for director of their three camps. The job was a mix of office work during the winter and outdoors during the summer, on site at the camps. I applied without thinking because it fit so perfectly with where I eventually wanted to be – outside.

During the interview process, some of the questions centered on how I could make this work for myself and for my family (with our three small children) – it's definitely not the same kind of job as being a lawyer with a startup and it is several hours from the Bay Area by car. It was basically a litany of questions designed to figure out if I was a long-term fit for this job as they did not want to be searching for a new director in a year or two if it didn't work out. Even though I was open to this wildly different opportunity because it fit where I wanted to go long term, the interviewers made a value judgment that I did not fit because they couldn't see beyond me raising three boys and my current career track.

Having a comprehensive work life and personal life vision makes it easier to make decisions. Ask yourself: does this fit with my vision or not?

Out of Balance

When your work life and personal life mix gets out of balance with where you want it to be, what then? When you start feeling like work is all you do or your personal life is interfering with your work, you may need to reassess your vision and your mix.

One exercise I share with clients is the T-Exercise, which will give you insight into what balance or imbalance you have between your reality and your vision. To do this exercise, draw a T down the middle of an entire piece of paper. Label one side of the T "Personal" and label the other side "Business." Each day for a week, keep track of three accomplishments each for business and personal activities. Only after you have done this for an entire week should you look at the information. Look for patterns, things that bother you, and overall mix between business and personal accomplishments. A sample T-Exercise is included here:

Personal	Business
Brought in mail, sorted it & put it away	Returned all outstanding phone calls
Meditated for 15 minutes	Paid monthly expenses
Walked the dog	Replied to unread emails

When my clients do this exercise, it is very evident on a daily basis that their work-life mix is off-kilter. As you take a longer view and look at a week, it may start to even out. The question isn't whether your work and life balances 50-50 like a teeter-totter. The question is – do you feel overwhelmed by either work or by personal obligations or both, or, do you feel things are working well. Doing this type of tracking of your work and personal accomplishments can give you very specific insight into your life as it is and your life as you envisioned.

This type of assessment and reassessment of where you are with your goals is about regret-proofing your life – the bucket list, the mix of work and life and how it fits into your vision – it's all about you. You are the designer of your own life – whether it's for work or play, you get to choose.

The quote at the beginning of this chapter is from page 163 of Chris Guillebeau's book, *The Happiness of Pursuit*, in which he quotes Stephen Kellogg, a musician, as saying: "It's better to be at the bottom of the ladder you want to climb than the top of one you don't." This statement is so true. If it feels right for you and your vision, don't let other people's ideas of what your life is supposed to look like (job, marriage, mortgage, kids) dictate your own goals or path. It's your own vision. Do what fits your wants and desires.

In summary, in Step 2 of the WELCOME Process, you have taken a closer look at what you want in your work life and your personal life and what that mix is. You have made a bucket list of things you want to accomplish in your lifetime. You may even have made a vision board to depict your work-life mix. Continually reassessing how you are doing will keep you on your path and help you get closer to reaching your goals. Once you have a good idea of what your vision is, you can compare where you are with where you want to be, which is covered in the next step.

More Resources

Books:
The Happiness of Pursuit by Chris Guillebeau

Movies:
"The Bucket List"
"10"

Research:
Dominican University Study
https://www.dominican.edu/academics/lae/
undergraduate-programs/psych/faculty/assets-gail-matthews/
researchsummary2.pdf

Exercises:
- Work-Life Vision – Answer these vision-defining questions to get a better understanding of what you want in your work life and your personal life
- Bucket List – List goals you want to accomplish in your lifetime
- Vision Board – Create a vision board (physically or electronically) to depict your goals
- T-Exercise – Examine your accomplishments at work and in your personal life.

These exercises are available at
www.sonyasigler.com/book_bonuses

A Work-Life Vision Workshop and a Vision Board Workshop are available on request at www.sonyasigler.com/workshops

Chapter 5:

Locate the Gaps

Fit Assessment/Gap Analysis

"Happiness depends on ourselves."
– Aristotle

Step 3 of the WELCOME Process explores how to locate the gaps between what you want in your career and what you currently have, what your role is and how much of a fit that role is for you based on your goals, and what it takes to get promoted where you are. Your career happiness and satisfaction are correlated directly to the size of the gap between what you want and what you have in your career. Can the gap be closed with small incremental changes or do you need to make a big sweeping change? It's time to find out.

Your Situation

First, as you evaluate your current situation, take a hard, honest look at where you are in your career. What is your current role? Is it what you thought it would be? Is it engaging or are you bored and check out? Do you feel stuck or frustrated? Do you manage people and love it or do you hate managing people and just want to do your job without managing people? Do you have to travel for your job and love it? Or do you hate to travel for work? Do you feel like you are being held back? Is your boss supportive? Take a hard look at what is driving you nuts or annoys you about your current situation. Take an equally hard look at what you like about your job. With a Pro/Con Exercise, write your notes into two lists – one for pros, the other for cons.

My client Belinda came to me because she was so frustrated with her job that she was ready to quit but felt she couldn't as the sole breadwinner in her family. She wanted to know whether she could make her current situation work or whether she needed to find another job. We worked together to make a critical assessment with a pro and con list of her current situation as general manager of a company with three different lines of business. She had worked herself into a trusted position with the founders, but one of the founders had slowly become jealous of the other founder to the point where he was having yelling fits and behaving badly.

This pro/con list was pretty stark. Both founders were board members; neither one was going anywhere. They all had to work together. Belinda loved most aspects of her job and had an amazing, trusted working relationship with the other founder. She loved managing the P&L, and she especially loved mentoring and nurturing the team she worked with. But she hadn't had a raise in several years. Her daily commute was over an hour and a half each way. Belinda's pro/con list was extremely revealing: (1) she had a job she loved; (2) she had a horrible commute; and (3) she had to work with a real jerk who made things very difficult for her to the point of harassment. Doing this same kind of pro/con assessment will help you get a realistic view of your current career situation.

Are You a Fit for Your Role?

Now that you have seen the truth of your current situation you can assess whether your role is a fit for you and your work and personal goals. Figuring out if you are a fit for your role will require you to look at your role, your team, and your company in more detail. Start with your role for a Locate the Gaps exercise.

Do you like the work you are doing? Is it exciting or challenging? Or are you bored just thinking about it? Are your skills a match for the role you are in? When you first start a job, you may have certain expectations for that role and company. Are those expectations being met or were they dashed when reality set in?

When I was in a CFO role at a startup, I was at first excited and challenged with putting in place the financial side of our company from scratch – setting up accounts payable and receivable and building out the time management and billing systems we needed. All that work was interesting and challenging at first. However, once the day-to-day work set in and I was doing the same set of tasks each month, I became frustrated and bored. I felt stuck. My skills center on making something from nothing and organizing chaos, not on the routine day-to-day tasks. If a role is not using your best skills, it may not be a good fit for you.

Do you like to come to work? If you pull into the parking lot at work, feel a pit in your stomach, and dread going in, then you need to take a look at why and make a change. Do you like your colleagues? Or do you have that one "impossible-to-work-with" coworker? Look closely at the alignment between your skills and your role to see if there is a fit.

One area that people usually discover a mismatch only once they are in a job is with the culture of a team or company. It is important to make sure your role is a fit with your own goals and values as well as those of your team and company.

One company professed to want people to plan ahead, work reasonable hours, and to not become workaholics. They encouraged people to go home by 6:00 p.m. Yet at every company and all-hands meeting, they would praise and reward people who went the extra mile by staying late, working the weekend, or handling something that had become a crisis. Instead of praising people for accomplishing their work on time or averting a crisis, they praised people who stayed those long hours or worked those weekend days. It was a mismatch between what they said they valued and what they actually valued.

One client, Darcy, worked at a company that sold their own services alongside their channel partners so that there was an inherent conflict in selling to certain clients. Their chief question was whether the company was going to sell directly to that client or whether the business was going to go through a channel partner. Darcy was constantly put into a position of stalling or holding off on things with customers because others, higher up, were trying to figure out whether they wanted to sell directly or let sales go through the channel partner. This put her in a constant position of acting at a different level of integrity than her own. It was a mismatch in values between Darcy's values and the values of the company.

Any value mismatch like this example from Darcy will lead to constant frustration and constant questions about why this is happening. You might hear yourself say, "I don't understand why this keeps happening." If you find yourself in this situation frequently, take a closer look at what the company really values and evaluate those values against your own for any incongruences.

While conducting a workshop for a women's networking group, the manager I was working with told me that her company supposedly supported the women's group. They touted their support in the press and in their marketing materials. But then she told me that the company never actually promoted any women even when there were plenty of qualified women at their company. In fact, during the latest round of promotions, others approached her and asked why she had not been promoted. It was a question she couldn't answer. The company management team only paid lip service to gender equality, with support of it in words, but not in its actions. If you value gender equality, then working at a company that acts like this is not going to be a value match for you. If you find yourself at a company like this, you need to reconsider whether you want to work for such a company.

What Does It Take to Get Promoted?

Once you've assessed your current situation and fit for your role, you can take a closer look at what it takes to reach the next level in your career. There are a lot of questions to consider as you take an honest look at getting promoted.

Do you know what is required to get promoted in your current position? Do you know what it takes to make a promotion happen at your company? Are you doing excellent work? Does your boss know about it? Are you sure? Does your boss' boss know about your work? Have you made your desire to be promoted known? Do you make your boss look good? What about your team? Do you make your team look good? Do people like to work with you? At all levels? Do others in the company know about your work?

Are you performing at the next level? Can you demonstrate that you can perform at that next level? For example, if you are required to manage a budget or people at the next level, can you do this work? Can you demonstrate that you can do this?

Do you have a clear understanding of how promotions work in your company? Do you need recommendations from others, or do you just need your own boss' support? All of these factors can play into whether you are promotable and whether it can happen in your current role and company.

If you are having trouble doing your own assessment to determine whether you are ready for the next level, you can take the quiz I have developed, which is on my website: www.sonyasigler.com/quiz.

At Intuit, I asked and couldn't get a straight answer on what it took to get promoted. I had no road map, other than to work hard, do good work, and keep working. That wasn't a formula to get promoted, that just led me to a point of frustration and burnout.

My client Edward told me that at his company managers must put together a specific package of support for anyone being considered for a promotion. This package must include support from the manager, a person at each of the next two higher levels, as well as current peers. It takes effort to put this package together. The easier you make it for your manager to put your name forth, the sooner a promotion is likely.

Another client, Frances, was vying for a position that would send her to Europe as an expat for two years. In Frances' own words, "I realized that I needed to understand how to motivate my own boss to give me what I wanted. At first, it just felt like sucking up to me, but then I had an aha moment when I realized that I had to make it easy for him to go to management and make this role change happen for me." To motivate your boss, you may need to appeal to his ego or support his goals.

At this point, you need to make an honest assessment about whether you can get promoted where you are. If the answer isn't "heck yes," how can you make it a "heck yes?" If you have a clear answer of what it takes to get promoted in your current role and company, then you should be doing everything you can to meet those goals. Otherwise, take a closer look at why you don't have that clarity.

Are you being caught in the political cross-fire between managers or teams? Are you at a company where there are constant reorganizations and you have to educate a new boss on what you do every time? That alone can slow down your career progress and any promotion process. Are there budget constraints? There are many other reasons why a promotion may not be on the horizon for you. Being aware of the situation and figuring out what to do about it are two different things.

What to Do About the Gap

Once you have identified any gap between your goals and where you are in your current situation, then you can start looking at making changes. Do you need to make big sweeping changes, like a complete job change? Or would smaller, more incremental changes be more effective?

Incremental changes can immediately improve a situation. Do you remember my client Belinda? Instead of leaving a job she loved, she decided to make some immediate incremental changes. She limited her contact with the jerk and no longer attended board meetings where he was present. She started working at home one day a week to ease the stress of commuting three hours a day. She asked for an immediate raise and got it. And finally, she started doing one thing on her goal list: she started studying to become a licensed real estate broker. These incremental changes dramatically improved her day-to-day work frustration and stress levels.

My work situation changed many times during the nine years I was at one job. My children were one, three, and four when I started that job. My husband had a job at a startup, had time off in between jobs, and then he had a job with a crazy travel schedule. I was able to change work schedules many times while at that company. At one point, I changed my schedule and pay to three-quarter time to make my childcare and spouses work-travel situation work better.

At another company, one of the people on my team had taken paternity leave. He and his wife were trying to figure out how to take care of their new baby without putting her in daycare. I suggested to him that he take his family leave time one day a week to be home with and care for his daughter. Don't be afraid to be creative. It was a solution that he hadn't thought to ask for – his exact response was – "I can do that?" Yes, sometimes you just have to ask for the change you want or need.

What incremental changes can you make? If you can't think of any, this is a perfect topic to brainstorm with a spouse, friend, or trusted colleague. But what happens if you can't make any incremental changes that will make a difference to your situation? Or what happens if your gap is so large that no change at your current job will make a difference?

If you come to the conclusion that you need to make a big change – for example, you may conclude that you are not in the right role or that you can't get promoted where you are so you need to find something else or make a bigger change. You may need to change roles within your company or change jobs altogether.

The last part of the gap analysis is to do a continual assessment or reassessment. This evaluation is not a one-and-done tool. You can do these steps anytime you are stuck in your career – or life, for that matter.

In summary, Step 3 of the WELCOME Process is to Locate the Gaps: take an honest look at your current situation, your role, and the fit between your goals and your role. If your fit is good, you are more likely to be satisfied with your job. If you have a small gap, you can make incremental changes to improve your situation. If the gap is too large, you will be at a high level of frustration, and you may need to make a more extreme change. The next step explores what you can do to prepare yourself to make that bigger change.

More Resources

Are You Ready for the Next Level? Quiz which can be found at www.sonyasigler.com/quiz

Exercises:

- Pros/Cons – Listing the pros and cons for a situation can be enlightening
- Locate the Gaps – Comparing what you want with what you have will reveal any gaps

These exercises are available at
www.sonyasigler.com/book_bonuses

A Work-Life Vision Workshop is available on request.
www.sonyasigler.com/workshops

Secret 2: Knowing Your Value Matters

The second secret to reaching the next level of your career is knowing your value matters. With or without your consent or cultivation, your personal brand is the story told to attract people to you.

Clearly articulating what you can do and what results you can achieve for others is key to getting promoted and landing your next job. If people don't know what you can do for them, they may see you as a networking contact but not as an asset. It's not just a matter of knowing your value as a strength or superpower; you must be able to convey your value and achievements to others through stories that are authentic, meaningful, and memorable.

When we were selling Cataphora and I was looking for my next role, I had such a variety of experience from the previous nine years that I had trouble articulating everything that I had achieved. I was getting interviews, but I wasn't getting any offers. My résumé was attractive, but I wasn't able to articulate my strengths and value in a way that made it clear how I could help the companies that interviewed me. It was frustrating, disheartening, demotivating, and it was a hit to my confidence level – not to my confidence in my skills, but to my confidence in finding another job that was interesting and challenging.

As I was clearing out my office, I realized the breadth of the work I had done, which spanned legal, finance, sales, client services, and operations. As I tossed paper into the shredder bin, I started keeping a list of accomplishments and achievements in each functional area. This list became the basis of the stories I would develop and share to illustrate the problems I had solved and which types of problems I could solve, as I interviewed with other companies.

I boiled down my overall strengths to a few skills that I could articulate succinctly and then go on to give examples in a conversation or interview situation: organize chaos, distiller, power advocate, and strategic thinker.

Trying to articulate these strengths requires stories and examples to share with others. I discovered the power of storytelling as I shared these stories with others in a way that was meaningful and memorable for them. People always have a "What's in it for me" mind-set. Sharing my strengths in a storytelling manner really helped answer the "What's in it for me" question.

The next two chapters break down what goes into knowing your own value and what it means for others.

- Chapter 6 covers Step 4 of the WELCOME Process – Call Out Your Strengths. You will discover what your strengths are and what these mean as part of your personal brand.
- Chapter 7 covers Step 5 of the WELCOME Process – Own Your Value. You will explore what your superpowers are and develop stories around those powers to share with others to attract them to you.

These two chapters detail the work required to know your value, which is the second secret to reaching the next level of your career.

Chapter 6:

Call Out Your Strengths

What Are Your Strengths?

*"If you don't know your worth, if you don't know y
our value, if you don't know how fantabulous you are –
it's going to be hard for other people to see it."*
– Kelly Rowland

Step 4 of the WELCOME Process is to call out your strengths. This chapter will cover what your strengths are and what these mean for you and the results you can obtain for others. You will do your own assessment to name your top strengths. Knowing your value is not to be confused with knowing yourself and your own values in Chapter 3. Your career value is gauged externally in terms of what results you can achieve for others.

Assessing Your Strengths

First, start by assessing your own strengths. You know yourself best. It should be easy to list your strengths. Don't overthink this part. Write down as many strengths as you can think of. If you are having trouble thinking of a list of strengths, then list what you consider your personality plusses. If you are still having trouble putting a list of strengths together, then list a few words that your family or friends or colleagues use to describe you.

A word about positive versus negative traits: When I work through this exercise with clients or workshop participants, sometimes the only words that people write on their list of strengths are negative words, like stubborn. I strongly encourage the use of the positive side of a trait rather than the negative one – this is, after all, about your strengths and putting your best foot forward to be promoted or to find a job. Instead of stubborn, are you persistent?

One of the things I hear often, mostly from women, is, "I'm just doing my job. I'm not even sure what my strengths are." If you are having trouble making a list of your strengths or you can't think of more than two or three strengths, then you can always use an assessment tool. My favorite tool is StrengthsFinder (now Clifton StrengthsFinder), which is based on Tom Rath's book StrengthsFinder 2.0. Each copy of his book includes a unique access code or you can take the online version of the assessment, for a fee. I use this book as a reference, so I like having my own hardcover copy of the book. Your strengths may change over time in terms of their ranking, but your top ones won't change that much overall.

The StrengthsFinder assessment involves answering a series of questions where you choose between paired words. Once you have completed these paired choices, your top five strengths will be revealed.

Or you can do your own self-assessment using the StrengthsFinder 34 Talent Themes. Choose the top five that you think apply to you:

Achiever	Futuristic
Activator	Harmony
Adaptability	Ideation
Analytical	Inclusiveness
Arranger	Individualization
Belief	Input
Command	Intellection
Communication	Learner
Competition	Maximizer
Connectedness	Positivity
Context	Relator
Deliberative	Responsibility
Developer	Restorative
Discipline	Self-Assurance
Empathy	Significance
Fairness	Strategic
Focus	Woo

There are many other assessment tools to use to reveal information about you. Common tools in addition to StrengthsFinder, are the Myers Briggs Type Indicator (MBTI) and DISC. MBTI is often used in business, especially when there is discord among team members. It is often casually referred to as a personality test. Understanding your results from this assessment will give you insight into your preferred way of working. DISC is also used in business and is a behavior assessment tool that industrial psychologist Walter Vernon developed based on the DISC theory of psychologist William Marston (who was also the creator of Wonder Woman). It centers on four personality traits – dominance, influence, steadiness, and conscientiousness.

While you could spend hours online searching and doing assessments, these three will give you plenty of information for use in knowing your value and coming up with examples to illustrate your strengths.

Once you have your list of strengths, come up with two to three instances of your work or experience that illustrate each one. For example, Ginger's strength is "Woo" (in StrengthsFinder terms), and her story to illustrate this strength was: "One of my top strengths is Woo. I used this strength to recruit and build out an entirely new sales team in less than three months at my last company."

Another story example, from Hannah: "My strength is lifelong learning. I love to learn new things and understand completely how things work. At one company, I learned everything I could about the movie industry and what we as a company needed to do as we moved into converting movies for one of our new products."

One more story example is from Inga: "My strength is competition. I love competing against others. It motivates me to do better, be better, to sell more, and to get higher customer ratings. I work really well when I have a pacing partner. Sales contests and making the President's Club are huge motivators for me. I have made the President's Club every year for the last six years."

The examples you create to illustrate your value should be personal to your interests and work experiences. The more examples you can create for your top five strengths, the easier it will be to choose an appropriate example to share your value with others when the time comes.

Perception Versus Reality

I have a view of myself, and it doesn't always match how others view me. When the gap between how I perceive myself and how other see me is so large that I do not understand my influence or effect in the workplace (or other places for that matter), then it can become a problem.

I used the F word in relation to the superintendent at a heated school board meeting. I heard from other members of my own board that I could be intimidating. It was definitely not how I wanted to be perceived in that setting. It was also definitely not a way for me to be effective in getting anything done with the school district or other groups and organizations.

I decided to do a little research to gauge how I was perceived in different areas of my life. I developed a list of adjectives that may or may not describe me and I sent the list to people I interact with in different aspects of my life. This exercise can be done in paper form or, as in my case, with a Google survey.

The Adjective exercise is simple – have people mark the adjectives that they think apply to you. There is an additional free-form question to ask which other words not on the list might apply to you, in their opinion.

Before this survey, I would have said my strengths were being a leader and a go-to person, as well as a person who gets things done, is persistent/tenacious, self-motivated, and can figure things out. I found the survey results to be enlightening and very helpful in molding the perception I wanted to cultivate.

The results revealed that the perception of my strengths, in order of frequency, were leader, hard-working, energetic, creative, entrepreneurial, productive, level-headed, and reliable/dependable. These were similar to my own list, and funny enough, *intimidating* wasn't mentioned. One word that floated to the top ten that surprised me was collaborative. I don't usually think of myself as collaborative, but I am perceived in the community as collaborative, despite dropping the F bomb at that school board meeting. When I asked others about that meeting, the common sentiment was that I was seen as passionate, not intimidating.

Remember my client Christine: she used this adjective exercise when she left the military to find a civilian job. She made a Word document full of adjectives that she handed to other people to fill out and return to her. When she interviewed at corporations and was asked the dreaded open-ended question "Tell me about your strengths," she pulled out her stack of responses and could say exactly what her strengths were, in the words of others. The words of others are more powerful than when you talk about your own strengths.

One of the negative words (or a word that could be perceived as negative) on Christine's adjective exercise results was *distractible*. She was able to address that as a perceived weakness when she was asked about her weaknesses in job interviews. Using the words of others can be more effective when you are going for a promotion or looking for a new job.

What Others Say about You

It is important to keep track of the good things people say about you at work. I recommend keeping a "Kudos" file. Anytime someone sends you an email or message that contains praise, appreciation, or a note of "good job," put it in a folder labeled "Kudos" or something else fun and memorable. I keep my Kudos file in Evernote. Yours could be an email folder or a folder on your hard drive. Make sure you keep it somewhere you can get to even if you aren't in the job you have now. Think of it as a permanent file for you and your use.

If a colleague praises you and thanks you for an awesome job on a project, ask them to send your boss a note and copy you on it. Direct, written praise carries more weight than does you telling your boss that so-and-so loved the work you did on this project. Most people are willing to send your boss a note like this, if asked. The key is, if asked.

There is a recommendation feature on your LinkedIn profile for this type of praise. If a colleague sent you a note of praise or said it to you in person, don't be shy about asking them to put it in a recommendation form on LinkedIn if it makes sense to post the praise on your profile.

For team leaders and managers: When I manage people, I keep a note in Evernote for each person and when someone sends me praise or says nice things about my team, I put their words in their note. It helps me when the time comes to give feedback or write their review. It is a simple, yet effective tool for keeping track of the good (and sometimes bad) information about their work.

In this step of the WELCOME Process you have pulled together a list of your value to others and selected examples of each from your own work and experiences. The work that you have done in this chapter around knowing your value is foundational, and these values and examples will form the basis of what you will use to share your value, which is what you will explore in more detail in the next chapter.

More Resources

Books:
StrengthsFinder 2.0 by Tom Rath (paid, for the book or online) - https://amzn.to/2U6fmUq
The 34 Talent Themes described in more detail:
https://www.gallupstrengthscenter.com/home/en-us/cliftonstrengths-themes-domains

Assessments:
DISC Assessment (free)
https://www.123test.com/disc-personality-test/

Myers Briggs – MBTI [paid or free]
https://en.wikipedia.org/wiki/Myers–Briggs_Type_Indicator#/media/File:MyersBriggsTypes.png

How to Fascinate - https://ea106.isrefer.com/go/getprofile/ssigler/

Other Assessments:
https://www.123test.com/all-tests/

Exercises

- Adjective List – Use this exercise to understand how others perceive you
- Kudos File – Keep a file of the appreciations and good things people say about you or share with you
- LinkedIn Recommendations – Ask for recommendations when someone says that you have done a good job or that they like working with you

> The Adjective List exercise is available at
> www.sonyasigler.com/book_bonuses

A Finding Your Value Workshop is available on request.
www.sonyasigler.com/workshops

Chapter 7:

Own Your Value

Illustrate Your Superpowers through Stories

*"Yes, in all my research, the greatest leaders looked
inward and were able to tell a good story with
authenticity and passion."*
–Deepak Chopra

In Step 5 of the WELCOME Process, "Own Your Value,"
you will explore what your superpowers are and how to develop
stories around those powers to share with others. If you can't
articulate your value concisely and effectively, how will others
know about what you can offer them? In Deepak Chopra's
words, you need to "tell a good story with authenticity and
passion." All of this reiterates Eleanor Roosevelt's words quoted
at the beginning of the book, "You must do the thing you think
you cannot do." Own your own value. Tell your own story. Tell
your authentic story, with passion.

Hiring and promotions happen because someone believes
your value is a match for the results they need to achieve. Have

you ever wondered why someone was promoted and not you? Was that person who talks a good game but doesn't really do anything promoted recently? If you pause for a moment and consider why this may have happened, you will realize that they conveyed their value – true or not – in a meaningful way to someone else. The person they convinced believes that promoting your "talker" colleague will help them achieve certain results.

Owning your strengths and superpowers and sharing stories about your achievements will help others see your value as well. Owning your story and being able to talk about your achievements and what you bring to the table is probably the most important factor for being promoted or landing your next job. The five questions below are essential for breaking down what "owning your story" means:

- What are your superpowers?
- What are your achievements that correspond to your top three to five superpowers?
- Can you talk comfortably about your superpowers?
- Have you written your story?
- What happens if you need to reinvent yourself?

Let's look at the components that go into owning your story in more detail.

What Are Your Superpowers

Do you know what your superpowers are? What are your unique skills and strengths described in terms of what you do? *Superpowers are your strengths put into action.* How do you describe what your resilience looks like? Sharing stories about your superpowers is key to getting noticed at work. Can you articulate your superpowers? What is unique about you?

Most people have a difficult time articulating what they are good at in a memorable way. One of the tools I use with clients is called the Every Job exercise. I have them write down every job they have ever had from baby-sitting to mowing lawns to delivering newspapers to running a lemonade stand to what they are doing now. I tell them to include everything – high school jobs, college jobs, and side hustles. All of it. They write down what the job was, what they loved about it, what they hated about it; how they got the job and why they left it; and the name of anyone who is a reference for that job. These answers form the basis of their superpower stories.

Once that information is gathered in one place, like an Excel spreadsheet or Word document, then we look over the entire list of work for repeating themes and traits. Inevitably an entrepreneurial streak will be visible, or another theme will be readily visible. Once you've done this exercise, identify three to five unique superpowers from this information on your work history.

When I was changing jobs and had to articulate what I could do for companies, I went through this exercise and came up with several superpowers:

- Organize chaos – I take on big, hairy, messy projects that others aren't willing to touch because they don't know how to approach the problem or where to start

- Distiller – I can digest an enormous amount of information and distill it down to its essence to share in plain English with others
- Power advocate – I am willing to marshal people and resources to take on the seemingly impossible and get it done
- Strategic thinker – I think in processes from the big picture through all the details from beginning to end. Operation snafus, no problem. You need to make that happen, no problem; I'll take care of it!

Putting my skills and strengths into superpowers made it easier for me to explain what I could do for others.

When my client Belinda went through this exercise, she realized that she loved to develop and implement processes and procedures to make things work better and more efficiently. She also loved to train and teach other people how to use these systems. It was clear from looking at her answers that the jobs she loved and was the happiest in were the ones in which she had the autonomy and authority to retool and implement system changes, and these jobs were all in the real estate industry.

In her current job as general manager, the job she had been considering leaving, she realized that she is doing that exact systems and training work she is amazing at. She loved that aspect of her job. She just dreaded working with that one board member who was a jerk.

The second takeaway after reviewing her answers was that she got almost every job from someone she knew, not from answering an ad or job posting. Belinda realized that if she really wanted to leave this job she loved because one person was making her miserable that her next job would likely come as a connection from someone she already knows. She realized that she needed to stop neglecting her network and make more of an effort to cultivate her relationships.

The most important takeaways for Belinda with the "Every Job" exercise were that she needed to develop her stories around these superpowers so that when she was cultivating her network, she could effectively communicate what she could contribute and what kind of results she could obtain as well as regain her confidence in her skills.

What Are Your Achievements

To start writing your story, one of the essential components is your achievements and accomplishments. Most women keep their head down and do their job. When asked to articulate their achievements, they say something along the lines of "I'm just doing my job. I haven't achieved anything." I know I used to say that until I tried to quantify the number of people I had trained.

To apply for a speaker slot at a conference, I had to quantify who I had presented to. Once I started looking closer at who I had trained, I discovered that I had trained over one thousand lawyers through my private corporate speaking events and a five-part webinar series. I also discovered that I had taught kids at every level, from kindergarten through high school, and adults from college to law school and professionals. That discovery gave me a more concrete way of describing my accomplishments.

When identifying experiences for each superpower, choose one or two stories to describe and illustrate the superpower in more detail. One cautionary note when choosing these experiences: make sure the work is your own, not that of your colleagues or boss. If you were part of a team, then be prepared to describe your role and your contribution, as well as how that impacted the whole project. You can always add that you are ready to take on a larger role now that you've seen how it's done and gained more experience.

Making a list of your achievements is a necessary part of being able to tell your story. You can do this in a variety of ways, but one of the easiest is to start with your résumé and list a few achievements for each job or role you have listed. Start with these and then you can dig deeper into work that isn't on your résumé, but that you might want to highlight, like volunteer or club work. List as many as you can.

Quantify your achievements if at all possible. How much did revenue increase? How many clients did you serve? How many agreements did you negotiate over what time period? This quantification is a factual observation about your achievements. If you don't know exact numbers, make your best guess. It will be useful information for developing your story.

Can You Talk about Your Superpowers?

One of the most common self-limiting beliefs that I hear when working with clients on their superpower and stories is that they can't talk about themselves. They are so uncomfortable. They say it feels like bragging. Culturally, it is a big no-no. The message they have heard all their lives is, "Don't stand out. Blend in." The list goes on.

Whatever the reason you give to not talk about yourself, it is doing you a disservice. It is holding you back. It is preventing you from reaching the next level of your career. It is preventing others from knowing about you and your work. Own your strengths, your superpowers, and your achievements.

What is the cost of you not owning your superpower and achievements? Are you missing out on the opportunity to make a connection with someone? Are you missing out on the opportunity to share your success? What is the cost of not making your value known?

Developing your stories around your superpowers and your experience is difficult to do for most people. For example, if you are at a networking event, can you actually articulate what you do in terms of the value you bring to the table? Can you answer that question without saying what your role is or what your profession is? Here's one of my examples:

Q: What do you do?
A: I'm a lawyer.

Kind of boring and if you aren't interested in lawyers, and now you may be thinking of excuses to make your exit.

Q: What do you do?
A: I'm a dogged advocate.

Now that's a much more interesting answer and invites follow-up questions about what that actually entails. Then I tell them about taking the group of students to the high school principal's office to get our band director fired.

Have you ever asked the "What do you do?" question and received an answer that made no sense? Then you ask the follow-up question, "But no, what do you actually do?" And you get an equally unhelpful answer a second time. When telling others about you and your work, you want to avoid those kinds of vague and jargon-filled answers.

When asked, Julia, one of my clients, would describe her business as, "I run a safety training company." Exhausted after a three-day conference, she was sitting at the hotel bar enjoying a moment of quiet when a guy sat down next to her and asked, "What do you do?" In her exasperated state after answering that question a million times over the prior three days, she blurted out, "I make sure people don't die!" Well, that answer definitely led to a more in-depth conversation of "What do you mean you make sure people don't die?" She ended up gaining a new client out of that conversation.

Julia blurted out information that was authentic and memorable. It was a powerful conversation starter. She followed it up, of course, with more detailed stories to illustrate exactly what she does for clients. These stories about her are powerful illustrations of the results she can obtain for clients. If she hadn't been able to talk about her superpower in such a memorable way, she would have missed out on gaining a new client.

Writing Your Story

To write your own story, use all the information you have related to your skills and superpowers. Your overall story will eventually include your image in pictures, your chapters spanning different time periods or roles or industries in your life, and your highlights of certain achievements or experiences. Think of your jobs as chapters and your achievements and accomplishments as your highlights. More details on how you will use your image, chapters, and highlights will be covered in Chapters 8 and 9. For this part of writing your story however, the emphasis will be on illustrating your superpowers through your stories.

Stories that are authentic and relatable are the most memorable. For example, the story Julia told about her safety training company related to her work as a life guard in high school. She looked back at her work experiences and observed, "I think my entire safety mind-set for my CPR business and my life started with being a lifeguard in East Oakland trying to make sure no one drowned or got shot."

The exercise I worked through with Julia was "Developing Your Brag" from my Authentic Personal Branding workshop. The focus with authentic personal branding is to be able to share your achievements and accomplishments with others without feeling like you are bragging. It was developed from an exercise in Peggy Klaus' excellent book, *Brag! The Art of Tooting Your Own Horn without Blowing It*.

Developing your stories, or bragologues, for each of your superpowers takes a few minutes, along with a lot of insight, which is why we did all the prep work around your value, your strengths, and your superpowers. The process is simple – take one to two minutes to answer each of these five questions:

1. What are your personality plusses?
2. What are your career successes?
3. What is the most interesting thing about you or that has happened to you?
4. What have you built?
5. How are you making a difference in other people's lives?

Try to list at least three to five items in each answer. For Question 5 about making a difference, you may have only one to two items for your answer. Don't worry about the exact count, just answer the questions quickly with what comes to mind first. Don't second guess yourself and put down what you think you should. If you are having trouble thinking of an answer, write down what others would say about you. See the sample worksheet for the first part of this exercise:

SAMPLE WORKSHEET

Your Career Mentor
By Sonya Sigler

Know Your Value Worksheet

Name: Sonya Sigler   Date: 6/14/18

- named my kids after Nat'l Parks

Fill in at least 5 items in each quadrant (add more if you want). Be broad in your thinking. Think
about accomplishments at work, home, or with volunteer activities.
- I grow orchids
- I'll talk to anyone

Personality Plusses (funny, persistent, etc.)	**Most Interesting Things About You** (I've driven across the country three times, by myself with my three children)
- funny — doer - engaging —crazy- - persistent willing - problem solver to try anything - inclusive → - connected © Sonya	⇐ Grew up on a farm — showed cattle ⇐ I play all the brass instruments ⇐ I teach beginning trombone → I've taught at all levels K - college to work/professionals - I am willing to get on stage and do just about anything to get a laugh
Career Successes - prod dev (Developed and built a finance department from manage from scratch for a $25M company) built from scratch [— filing system @ VeB Dev office - finance billing/collections - HR, Sales, Client Services Legal - write all the time - teach everywhere - online banking - quicken mortgage - not afraid to take on projects	**What Have You Built?** (A loving, calm, and peaceful household) outside - $25 m company w/o investment ★ amazing network - fun friends, who love each other - backyard sanctuary - garden - 3 productive, funny kids - an amazing marriage - an amazing support system - an organized life - travel around the world

Know Your Value Worksheet

How have you made a difference?

Describe at least three scenarios where you have made a difference. Use metrics if possible (i.e. Managed all technology for 24,000 employees, managed a budget of $25M, built a sales team of 12 people from the ground up, while exceeding sales targets each year for five years).

- tell people I love them
- note of thanks, sympathy, gratefulness, hello
- remember people
→ authentic interactions (scares some, others gravitate towards it)
- coached kids / taught kids
- spoke my mind — Grace, Lynette, Damka

if someone has made a difference please let them know

Reread your answers above and fill in any others you may have forgotten, especially if you have had several jobs or roles. What catches your attention? Do you see any themes between the quadrants?

- crazy
- connected — people, information
- coaching / inspiring others
- systems
    - writing / sharing knowledge

Write down the top three items that resonate with you. (These items will be used in the next exercise to develop specific brags about you).

1. ___connected___
2. _____
3. _____

From your answers, look for themes or particular superpowers for which you want to develop a brag or story. In a workshop, attendees usually develop at least two brags. I recommend developing brags for each area of achievements for you because you are trying to get promoted or if you do decide to quit your job, you will need even more material to pull from as you interview for a new job.

These brags will be a *work in progress*. Don't worry about what they look like after your first attempt. There is always an opportunity to wordsmith and edit your brags. Adding in humor and childhood examples make your brags funny and more memorable. The point of these brags and stories is to get someone to remember you and to spark their interest in knowing more about you. It is the beginning of a conversation.

Sample Brags

Sample brags include:

- Hi, I'm Ed. I'm a biochemist. I'm the kid who got a chemistry set for Christmas at age six and never stopped playing with it. Now I do research for one of the world's largest pharmaceutical companies.
- I am not afraid of hard work. I helped develop a business from nothing to a million-plus-dollar company within three years.
- I like to think of myself as a "flame fanner." I can see the spark inside people, and I use my words as bellows to help them see the fire and passion inside them.
- My name is Kathryn. I am equally at home in Silicon Valley and on stage at the Symphony Hall. The same discipline that put me on stage at Carnegie Hall got me an MBA at MIT. I love making things better, whether it's a performance on stage or a business process.
- I'm a master organizer. I am so organized I have my personal movie collection in an Excel spreadsheet. Her prior one: I'm an organized and detail-oriented project manager.

- I'm a master historical costumer. I use my insane obsession with history and my mad sewing skills to provide textile time travel for the discerning reenactor.
- I work with people who want to make their dreams come true. I help them plan now for a financially sound future so they can live their dream life. Her prior one: I'm a Financial Planner.
- My name is Laurie, and I once rescued a cockatiel from a movie parking lot. Now I rescue recruiters by coordinating and organizing their candidates and interviews.
- I am a connector and bridge builder – of people, concepts, ideas, anything! With my international background and experience across a dozen industries, I have helped grow businesses and people in ways they had not realized was possible.
- My name is Mitchell. I make CEOs human. Over my twenty-year CEO consulting practice, I have saved dozens of marriages.

One of the first bragologues I developed when I did this exercise was: "I am a startup magician. I help companies start something from nothing. I work with startups to help them grow." Then I looked at my experience from this perspective, and I realized I help larger companies do this as well. At each company, I gravitated toward the new business groups, the ones innovating and inventing something that didn't exist before. That's when I realized I have the "figure-it-out" gene, as in "I don't know how this will work, but let's figure it out." See the sample from one of the first "brags" I developed:

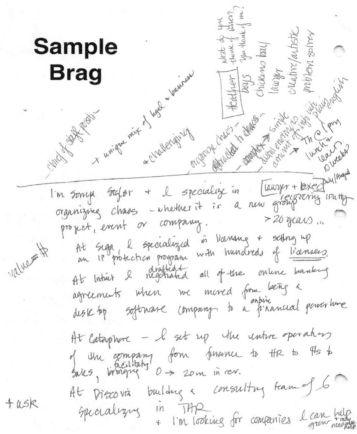

Sample Brag

After developing my story further and in more detail, I added a story about organizing chaos and this one about being a master organizer: "I am a master organizer. I can organize anything from your garage to your company. I think my obsession with organizing things started at a very early age when I alphabetized my books in grade school. My mom loves to tell everyone that I was voted best organized in kindergarten." Obviously, there is more to this story, and I can pull out more examples if I am in a situation where I need to share more details or explain my specific experience.

As you develop your brags, look at your experience and add stories related to your experience – whether in a job or throughout your life. These stories will make you more relatable in general and especially when you are networking or interviewing.

Over the next week as you find yourself in situations answering the "What do you do?" question, try out your brag. See how it feels. Adjust it if necessary, listen to the reactions and feedback from others. The stories you are telling around your superpowers will sound awkward at first when you start speaking them. It will get easier. It usually takes six times of saying it until you reach a comfort level where it sounds easy and natural.

These brags can also form the basis of your bio or introduction. Julia has incorporated more of her stories into her CEO bio, and she now uses this one when she is introduced for keynotes or other presentations: "Julia is the girlfriend you want seated in the emergency exit row on your plane." Developing your own brags is a process of drafting, improving, practicing, and repeating the process.

Reinventing Yourself

A word about reinventing yourself when you find that you are stuck in your career. Reinvention is an extension of where you are now and where you have been. You might be doing something completely new like changing from being a tax accountant to selling real estate. In any event, your reinvention will involve the exact same work that I just described in this chapter, except this time you will be doing it with an eye toward identifying transferrable skills.

One client, Meredith, was thinking about applying for an executive director position at a nonprofit. She would be leaving her environmental consulting practice but didn't know how best to approach it. We did a VIP day and broke down the job description for the executive director position and then we went through the "Every Job" exercise before categorizing her skills and strengths. We matched up all of her skills to each one of the areas required for the executive director position. Then we developed detailed stories around each skill set to illustrate her experience and knowledge in that area. It gave her specific stories from her experience to talk about when she was asked about it in interviews. The underlying work about owning her value and telling her stories led to her getting that executive director position.

All of the work you have done in this chapter illustrates your superpowers so that you can now share your value with others concisely and effectively.

Now, in the next step, you will learn how to share your value with others.

More Resources:

Books:
Brag! The Art of Tooting Your Own Horn without Blowing It by Peggy Klaus
https://amzn.to/2EyH2fl

Exercises:

- Every Job – List every job you ever had to gain insight into your skills and superpowers
- Developing Your Brag – Develop your stories to illustrate your superpowers

These exercises are available at
www.sonyasigler.com/book_bonuses

An Authentic Personal Branding – Be Known for Who You Are Workshop is available on request at
www.sonyasigler.com/workshops

A Storytelling to Get What You Want –
Perfecting Your Pitch Workshop is available on request at
www.sonyasigler.com/workshops

Secret 3: Sharing Your Value Matters

The third secret to reaching the next level of your career is to share your value with others. You have to get over your reluctance to be known and take personal responsibility for what others know about you inside and outside of your company. Being able to share your value with others is key to being known within your company and outside your company, whether in your industry or beyond.

When I was at Discovia, the team I led participated in an industry study. It was a long and involved but very strategic study that took months and months of extra time and effort to complete. When the results were shared with us, our team was the only team that scored in the top five in all three of the judged categories. Our company celebrated our success; my team celebrated our success; my boss celebrated our success; and I celebrated our success. My team was cheered at the next all hands meeting for our company. But I bet if you asked other teams throughout the company what we did, they couldn't have described the study or what we had done in it.

Being known for leading this study was great, but it was only half the story. Writing up the details of our participation and each person's role in the study and sharing it with the rest of the company was an important part of that participation and success. I wanted to make sure every person in the company knew about our extraordinary accomplishment – for me and for every member of my team. I wanted them, as well as myself, to be known for what we had done in detail for our submission and what we had accomplished. It was important because the work we had done for the study was the same work we did on a day-to-day basis for our clients. This last step of communicating internally was closure for the project we had completed, and it made the connection for others on how the work could be used with clients.

I wanted others in the company to know what my team could do for them and our clients. It was important to spread the word about how talented they were as search and retrieval consultants and what we could do with our latest data analytics software. Unfortunately, because of the terms of the study, I couldn't publish anything externally until the authors of the study published the results (which we are still waiting on). It would have been even more powerful and effective if we could have shared our study performance with clients and others in the industry, not just for me, but for my team members as well.

The next two chapters explain what goes into sharing your value with others inside and outside your company.

- Chapter 8 covers Step 6 of the WELCOME Process – Make Yourself Known Internally. You will explore how to make yourself, your work, and your accomplishments known internally at your own company.
- Chapter 9 covers Step 7 of the WELCOME Process – Externally Become Known. You will explore how you can become known outside of your company, throughout your industry, or beyond.

These two chapters detail the work required to share your value, which is the third secret to reaching the next level of your career.

Chapter 8:

Make Yourself Known Internally

Be Known Inside Your Company

*"To succeed in this world you
have to be known to people."*
– Sonia Sotomayor, *My Beloved World*

Step 6 of the WELCOME Process explores how to make yourself, your work, and your accomplishments known internally at your own company. Several areas will be covered: who knows your work; how to cultivate support; how to make your work known; and make the ask.

Who Knows Your Work

To make an honest assessment, take a broad look at who knows about your work. Look up and down the management chain and at your colleagues. Also look at other groups within your company that you work with. Start with your boss and assess what she knows about your current projects, past achievements, and skills that you may not be using in your current role. You can do this in a casual conversation or a more formal one-on-one meeting.

In the study example I described earlier, my boss knew exactly what we were doing because I kept him updated constantly as it was all extra work for me and my team. But I would have bet that other groups in the company could not have articulated much about me or my team's participation in the study and what our company had contributed. It's not surprising. Everyone is busy doing their own work. There is very little opportunity to learn about other's work unless your work is dependent on that other person or group. For the study, I could have said, "Wow! We just turned in our study submission after three months of hard work in addition to our day-to-day work."

Have the same casual conversation with your team colleagues and then branch out to other groups that you work with. You can ask, "I'm doing a little research into who knows about my work. How much do you know about what I do?" Or "Tell me in your own words what it is you think I do." Whether you receive a vague or specific answer, you can dig a little deeper into what other people know about your work through these personal conversations.

To get a complete picture of how extensively (or not) that your work is known in the company, you can have a similar conversation with people up and down the management chain. It can be a simple question, "Do you know what I do? Or what our group does? I am trying to get a better understanding of how widely known our work is in the company." Of course, you'll need to be able to describe what you do if they have no idea or a vague idea. Keep that description short and cover the highlights that you do want everyone to know.

Making an honest assessment about who knows your work and achievements will give you a better idea of what relationships you need to cultivate and who you need to inform about your work.

How to Cultivate Support

First of all, it goes without saying, but I find that I need to remind clients occasionally, to make sure that the work you do is excellent. Be excellent. Then make your excellent work known beyond you, starting with your boss. Your boss may have an idea of what projects you are working on, but not many others will.

When it comes to communicating your work to your boss, make sure you close the communication loop. My client Nancy felt like her boss was starting to micromanage her. The problem boiled down to a lack of communication about an important project. Her boss was being asked questions by higher-ups he couldn't answer. He, in turn, would ask Nancy what was going on – even though it was something she had already taken care of. She hadn't closed the loop with her boss to make sure he knew it was done. All it takes is a simple email, text, or IM to close the communication loop.

Being known more widely internally is just as important for cultivating support, if not more important than external networking. The context for the Sonia Sotomayor quote from *My Beloved World* at the beginning of this chapter is networking. "Sometimes, idealistic people are put off the whole business of networking as something tainted by flattery and the pursuit of selfish advantage. But virtue in obscurity is rewarded only in Heaven. To succeed in this world you have to be known to people." Your work has to be known to others. Communicating your value to others is an important part of your success.

Relationships matter – whether it is with your boss or colleagues or other groups in your company. How are you managing or cultivating those relationships? Do you have mentors (formal or informal) in your company? How often do you talk to your mentors? Do they know what your achievements are? Sharing an achievement is making you known, not letting you languish in obscurity. Sharing your work can be as simple as saying, "Wow, I am glad that project is finally finished. I worked really hard to make sure it was completed on time and on budget." Now you have planted a seed in other people's minds that you bring projects in on time and on budget and that you are a hard worker. It may seem awkward at first when you share your achievements with others, but it will become more comfortable the more you share.

If you have a sponsor – someone who is actively championing you and your work – you definitely want to make sure that person knows your skills, strengths, and achievements whether the achievements were from your current company or not. You want your value known to your sponsor so he can spread the good word about you.

Cultivating relationships up and down the management chain is important for two reasons. First, cultivating a relationship with higher-ups makes you known and familiar instead of an unknown when your name comes up for a promotion. Second, people below you will be your future team members when they are promoted. Knowing both is helpful.

Excellent customer and vendor relationships also play an important part of being known internally. Any customer that says to your boss, "I love working with Sonya" is worth their weight in gold. When someone other than you says good things about you, it carries more weight than when you talk about yourself.

Cultivating these relationships throughout the company and with your customers and vendors requires face time or phone time. You can leave your desk and cultivate relationships by walking around. Or if you work remotely or don't have an office conducive to walking around, you can pick up the phone and call people. Leaving everything to email or text can lead to a vague understanding of what you do. I'm reminded of the Maya Angelou quote, "I've learned that people will forget what you said, people will forget what you did, but people will never forget how you made them feel." Get out of your office and make a personal connection to cultivate your company relationships.

How to Make Your Work Known

You can tout your work or others can tout your work and achievements. Why not do both? You can share your work with others in a casual, conversational manner: "I just finished writing up a case study on how our customer used this little-known feature in our product. Who do you think needs to know about this?" or a completely different conversation: "What would make your job easier?" Listen to the answers closely, and they will guide you on what work and achievements to make known.

One client, Christine, who worked at a global communications company, would send out an email every Friday to her boss, copying two levels above her boss, plus her team. She would describe at least one thing that she had completed that week, where on the server to find the article or presentation (or whatever it was), and how it was being used, by what team and in what context. At the end of the year, not only had Christine shared her value and achievements with others, but she also had a good record of her achievements.

One of the questions I hear when we talk about copying your boss or higher-ups is "What if your boss thinks you are going over his head when you send an email like that?" First, I would send it anyway and address any issues with the truth, "I thought you would want others to know what I/our group was working on." If you think that won't fly with your boss (for whatever reason), then ask permission. I usually err on the side of asking for forgiveness, not permission, but that is my personal style. You will need to do what works best for you and the corporate culture you are in.

As a lawyer, I never felt like I had anything to tout. I was just doing my job, supporting my clients. Looking back at my early roles, I could have sent my boss and the business group higher-ups a weekly update of where we were on negotiations or the deal approval process. This type of communication and closure makes sure people know you have everything handled. The power of closing the loop or over-communicating cannot be underestimated.

It is even more powerful if others share your work and achievements. One example I love is from the Obama administration women who worked closely together in the White House. They would tout each other's ideas through amplification – repeating another woman's idea using the prior woman's name in conjunction with the idea. This precluded men from claiming the idea as their own. They were trying to replace gender inequity in how women's ideas were listened to and how their contributions were known. The way they went about it was powerful because they were sharing someone else's ideas.

This kind of sharing can be done in meetings – merely thanking someone for their work on a project can bring her contribution to light in front of others. It is simple to make this type of showcasing of other's achievements a regular practice, especially if you manage a team. You want your team's work to be widely known.

You may have to network more specifically inside your company if you want skills that you aren't using in your current job to be known by others. This issue comes up in the context of lateral moves or promotions. You may not be known for project management that you did in the past if you are currently in a different role. In this case, you will do some education for the managers you want to know about your project management skills. Have a direct conversation with that manager while at the same time, start mentioning to others the prior projects you worked on as a project manager.

For example, in my first two jobs as a lawyer, I spent a lot of time working on the due diligence process for acquisitions. When I started working with startups, I wasn't doing that type of due diligence work any longer, but when we decided to sell the company, we definitely were going to go through a due diligence process. Bringing up my acquisitions experience was relevant at that point.

I had one client, Olympia, who faced this type of obstacle at her company. Although she was perfectly happy staying in her role and growing, she was really energized by a different role altogether. When she applied for this other role, no one internally knew she had that type of experience at prior companies. Yes, that experience was listed on her résumé, but no one looks at your résumé internally after you are hired. In her current company, Olympia wasn't known for that particular work experience. She had to educate the hiring manager and others in a position of influence.

You will have to network internally to be known and to share your value. If you are working in a remote or global situation, you will need to be even more strategic and diligent in your networking efforts as the "out of sight, out of mind" phenomena is widespread. You will have to work harder to make yourself and your achievements known in a remote or dispersed working environment.

Make the Ask

You will be making some kind of an ask to reach a higher level in your career – whether it is for more responsibility, a raise, a promotion, or for a new job. There are several components to making an ask: knowing the outcome you want, knowing your audience, and sharing your value that matters to that audience.

The work you did in figuring out who you are and what you want is a fundamental building block along with illustrating your skills and your superpowers with your story. Developing the confidence to be bold, stand out, and get the attention you deserve requires you to share your story with others.

If you want to be promoted, you will need to demonstrate that you have taken on more and more responsibility and can operate at that higher level. You won't get that opportunity by sitting back and keeping your head down. You won't be handed a promotion. You get that opportunity by asking. Ask to take on the hard projects. Volunteer yourself, don't wait to be asked. If you want a different role in the company, making your desires known early and often is the way to plant the seeds in others minds that you want that position. Making your ambitions known makes it easier for others in power to know what you want and where you want to go with your career.

Let's talk specifically about your audience. Telling your story to others will place you front in center in their mind. But who will you address? If you are asking for more responsibility, then your audience will be your boss. If you want to speak to a higher level of managers in your company or stand in for your boss at a meeting or conference, then you will be asking your boss. If you are vying for a promotion, your boss will be your primary audience, plus whoever else to be convinced in your own company – every company handles promotions differently. Some companies require support from two levels up and lateral groups. Know who your specific audience is.

If you have discovered in your gap analysis that it is unlikely you will be promoted in your current position, then your audience will be a hiring manager – either elsewhere in your company or in another company altogether. Using the stories you developed in chapters 6 and 7, you will be able to share your value, your achievements with the hiring manager, as well as anyone else in your network.

Helping yourself is as simple as sharing your value with others, starting with those in your own company. Making a change to reach the next level of your career requires you to share your value through stories. If you have concluded that you cannot get promoted in your current company and that you need to make a move, the good news is that the work you have done to make yourself known internally is equally applicable outside of your company.

More Resources

Books:
My Beloved World by Sonia Sotomayor
https://amzn.to/2T2BAdK

Articles:
"Obama's Female Staffers Came Up with a Genius Strategy to Make Sure Their Voices Were Heard" by Claire Landsbaum. Sept. 13, 2016. https://www.thecut.com/2016/09/heres-how-obamas-female-staffers-made-their-voices-heard.html

Exercises:

There are no written exercises in this chapter. You actually need to get out of your office and talk to people. Or if you work remotely, communicate with others in your department or company, if only to find out what they are working on. Lastly, who needs to know about your work? Talk to them about your work this week.

Are You Ready for the Next Level? Quiz available at
http://www.sonyasigler.com/quiz

A Mentors and Why They Matter Workshop is available by request at www.sonyasigler.com/workshops

An Anatomy of a Raise Workshop is available on request at www.sonyasigler.com/workshops

Chapter 9:

Externally Become Known

Be Known Outside Your Company

*"We can easily forgive a child who is afraid
of the dark; the real tragedy of life is when [wo]men
are afraid of the light."*
– Plato

This chapter covers Step 7 of the WELCOME Process, "Externally Become Known," and explores becoming recognized outside of your company, throughout your industry, and beyond. Becoming known outside your company or industry will raise your profile if you are interested in becoming a thought leader in your industry or if you can't get promoted where you are and need to find another position.

Keeping Your Résumé Current

Keeping a current résumé is a must, no matter how happy you are in your current job. You may need to send it out quickly when an opportunity presents itself. Don't wait to be asked for your résumé to update it for the last few years! Make sure your current role is detailed and your achievements are listed in your résumé.

If you don't list achievements in your résumé, you might want to keep a comprehensive list in an Excel or Word document or Evernote or some similar tool. When you need to write a cover letter you will have the information consolidated and ready to use.

If you are interested in a position that is different than your current role and you need to highlight transferrable skills, it may make sense to create a function-focused résumé (marketing experience) rather than a role-specific résumé (director of marketing). My client Meredith needed to update her résumé urgently because she was vying for a position that wasn't at all like her consulting position even though the same skills were used in that new position. She ended up retooling her résumé to match the functions required for the executive director position. She broke down her experience to match the functions rather than listing her roles and work experience under each role.

You may want to keep two or more résumé versions if your skills fit into vastly different areas. When the headhunter asked me, "Do you want to be general counsel or COO?" I realized I needed to highlight different experience for each position, and I developed two different résumés.

The stories that you share to illustrate your strengths and superpowers can be broken down into chapters and highlights to cover certain jobs or certain functional experience, whether it is based on certain roles or a certain industry or industries. In Meredith's situation, she highlighted stories illustrating her experience in leadership, fundraising, community collaboration, and volunteer recruitment. Even though she didn't have executive director experience in a position with that title, she had all of the functional experience from her various work and volunteer experiences.

If your experience varies to cover multiple industries or functions, you can write your stories as kind of chapters – regulatory, government, sales, etc. If you can catalog your stories, they will be ready for you to use as you need to share them on your search for a new position.

Not only do you need to keep your résumé updated, but you also need to keep your headshot current. There is nothing more disconcerting when the person who shows up for the interview looks nothing like their picture.

Managing Your Public Persona

Your public persona across platforms should be aligned. If you have a LinkedIn profile and a website, those stories should consistent with one another or there should be an explanation in the "About You" section of your website for why there is a difference.

Your public persona includes the pictures and images you use. Are these images professionally done or did you pull a picture of you from your friend's Facebook feed or your last vacation? The images you use should all convey the same aligned message. You might need to have new headshots taken that convey the message you want to send out.

I have one client, Abby, who was trying change her position at her company to get promoted to a senior level and at the same time become a sought-after keynote speaker. She retooled her image across every platform in which she appeared, starting with LinkedIn. She had new headshots taken and she had more photos taken at her speaking events to show the large audiences at her talks. These images were aligned with her goal of doing more keynote speeches along with finding a new job.

The stories you are telling should align with your images, any articles you are writing, and any items on which you are commenting. Whether it is a hashtag or a message or an image – all of it should align with your message and your story.

LinkedIn is a flexible platform from which to shout your message. Your profile doesn't have to be a regurgitation of your résumé. I advise my clients to use ALL of the "real estate" provided in LinkedIn – from the header picture to the recommendations and events. I urge my clients to put authentic information and goals on their profile. People visiting your profile will know what you are looking for and what you are focused on.

If you are open to being contacted by recruiters, then make sure that is activated on your LinkedIn profile. You can specify that you are happy in your current position and are open to the solicitation. There are other designations available for this contact function.

Take a look at how you appear across all of the platforms – whether Facebook, Twitter, Instagram, or another platform. Is it aligned? Do you need to make changes and updates? Companies use these platforms to do reference checking and look for any potential issues. Make sure you are depicting the story and the image that you want to convey.

Thought Leader Activities

If you want to be known outside your company, you will be doing writing and speaking and other networking activities to build your network, profile, and expertise. What do you want to be known for? What are you an expert in? There is a very useful book written by Denise Brosseau, Ready to Be a Thought Leader?, that will guide you through the process of becoming an industry expert and a go-to person

As the Federal Rules of Civil Procedure were updated and changed in 2006, I presented on those changes and the impact. I gave hundreds of presentations. As various data analytics software and technology were deployed to help companies (and their lawyers) to comply with the 2006 rule changes, I could talk about that in detail. I could explain the technology in plain English – not only to users, but also to lawyers who had to sign off on using the new technology.

I built a niche of explaining the technology in plain English and being able to train lawyers in linguistics and statistics (not many lawyers went to law school to study statistics). I've trained thousands of lawyers in data analytics. I didn't start out to become an expert in this area but that is what happened with educating lawyers about the law changes and the impact.

This thought leader activity included writing blogs and articles – all of which were aligned with becoming a data analytics expert and helping to demystify the technology used in a context new to lawyers. Gravitating toward trends and hot technology (think blockchain and cryptocurrency) will give you more visibility.

As you build your expertise and become known within your industry, you will need to develop a speaker sheet and other presentation materials, like a bio and speaker photo. Keep these materials up-to-date – from your image to your stories that illustrate your superpowers in different contexts.

Apply for awards. Whether self-nominated or not, apply for any and all awards that fit with your goal of being known and recognized for your work. Some awards are pay-to-play and require a company sponsorship, like paying for a table of 10 at the award dinner. Others are more merit and action based. Regardless, apply for awards and get the recognition you deserve!

Preparing to Make a Move

You will need to keep up-to-date: your résumé, your stories illustrating your superpowers, and your network. I can hear you now: "Ugh! I hate networking!" There is value in continuous networking, not just when you are looking for a job. If you wait until you are looking for a job, people will think two things: (1) "She only calls when she wants something"; or (2) "I have no idea what she has been doing for the last five years." Neither of these are good.

Your networking can be general and friendly – "Hey, I wanted to give you a heads up about what I am working on these days." Or it can be more specific – "Hey, I wanted to let you know that I am giving a talk on fraud detection through pattern analysis these days. If you know of anyone who might be interested, please let me know." Your conversation will vary if you get someone on the phone or if you leave a voicemail. Either way, you can let people know what you are doing.

One of the techniques I used since I began my career is to lay out 5 business cards on the top left section of my desk each Monday. Over the week, I would contact each person to reconnect with them. Some weeks, I would contact all 5 people in one day. Some weeks I would contact one person a day. The result of this active network cultivation over the years is that people pick up the phone when I call. Whatever method you choose to cultivate your own network with is not important. The mere fact that you are actively cultivating your network is what is important.

The value of continuously networking cannot be understated. When I sold a patent portfolio, I found the broker who helped us sell our portfolio through a connection I made in the stands at one of my son's baseball games. You never know when someone will be hiring or if you can connect people in your network or help someone find their next job. You'll want that same courtesy when you are next looking for a job or other referral. Cultivating your network a little bit each day won't make it seem like such a monumental task.

Practicing the art of the ask is, indeed, an art. You'll get more comfortable with it the more you ask. Letting other people help you and, in turn, helping them when they need it is very satisfying. In this networking effort, don't forget the work you did in the last chapter internally in your own company. Networking internally and externally is the same type of effort – connecting with others, sharing your stories.

Once you start looking for a job outside your current role – whether it is for a different role in the same company or a new role altogether outside your company, you will need to convey your value and your stories will do just that. All of the work you have done through this WELCOME process builds on the prior steps. Step 7 is the culmination of having a goal, knowing your value, and sharing your value.

More Resources

Books:

Ready to Be a Thought Leader?: How to Increase Your Influence, Impact, and Success by Denise Brosseau, Foreword by Guy Kawasaki

https://amzn.to/2Vjl3P4

The Art of Asking: How I Learned to Stop Worrying and Let People Help by Amanda Palmer, foreword by *Brene Brown*

https://amzn.to/2tFoiEL

Exercises:

- Current Résumé – Is your résumé current? If not, bring it up to date with recent roles and achievements.
- Networking – Assess your current network and networking efforts. Identify places where you can network and make a plan to go to those events and connect with others.
- Aligned Public Persona – is your public persona aligned with your personal brand and message that you want to

convey about yourself? If not, take steps to align every part of your public persona.

Are You Ready for the Next Level? Quiz
www.sonyasigler.com/quiz

A Getting Noticed on LinkedIn Workshop is available on request at www.sonyasigler.com/workshops

Chapter 10:

The Top Obstacles That May Still Get in Your Way

"There is no passion to be found playing small –
in settling for a life that is less than the one
you are capable of living."
–Nelson Mandela

I had an epiphany while I was writing this book. I gave a talk at the beginning of 2015 that I thought should be turned into a book. I have tried to write that book for the last four years – very unsuccessfully. I had a lot of quotes, research, pictures, and text all collected in a mishmash, but I had no clear view into what message I wanted to share and with whom.

Enter Angela Lauria and The Author Incubator, who offered a program after my own heart: it required learning and homework with very important deliverables. It was the right combination of learning and work pushing me to actually put pen to paper – or hands to keyboard, in my case – to get this book written and into your hands. It required clarity – what is your message and to whom? It required me to have a goal. Sound familiar?

One morning while I was lying in bed, I was trying to decide whether to get up and write, as I had diligently entered into my calendar for the day; or, if I should get up and go exercise outside, in the pouring rain; or, if I should snuggle with my husband and try to go back to sleep. I realized as I was trying to decide – holy cow – it isn't really about writing the book so much as keeping agreements with myself. To write the book, to get up and exercise, to do what I said I would do, for myself – I realized this book was about keeping agreements with myself. Do what you said you were going to do, for yourself.

That's exactly what this book is for you – it is about keeping your agreements with yourself to take control of your career situation, to ask for and get help, and, ultimately, to make a change.

When you can't keep an agreement with yourself to do what it takes to make a change, you've hit an obstacle. I continued to hit my head against that obstacle for over three years when it came to writing this book.

There are many obstacles that can get in your way. What do these other obstacles look like? I will highlight a few of them so you can recognize which ones might get in your way, despite your best intentions to commit to yourself and do the work required to change your narrative and make a change.

Thinking Small

When I first start working with clients, one of the things that is clear from the beginning is that they are thinking small.

They need a professional makeover to think bigger, to trust themselves, to rebuild their confidence, to rely on themselves. It starts with one step at a time.

Understanding their skills and strengths is an important step to (re)building the confidence they need to think bigger. Once we start going through their experience and putting their stories together, they gain the confidence to take a step forward to making a broader change.

Sometimes this thinking small mind-set takes a bit of work to uncover. The self-sabotage – the thinking small, the acting smaller – can be a deeply engrained habit that takes a bit of effort and action to change.

What does thinking small look like? It looks like settling. It looks like putting up with questionable behavior. It looks like tolerating behavior that is in opposition to your own values. It looks like lack of clarity on what the next steps are to being promoted. It looks like a lack of confidence in your skills and your ability to find another job. This thinking small mind-set can easily get in your way from moving forward to the next level of your career.

My client Belinda was used to thinking small and had been (figuratively) beaten down to think in a much smaller way. She had been belittled, questioned, shamed, and embarrassed in front of others in an office she was in charge of. This behavior undermined her confidence in her own abilities and in her ability to seek other opportunities elsewhere. It left her thinking, "I can't do any better elsewhere," which was completely untrue.

Trusting Others Instead of Yourself

Listening to others instead of yourself can get in the way of moving forward or implementing changes you say you want to make. Clients who listen to others instead of themselves have stopped trusting their own instincts and intuition. They start listening to others who don't know them well. They start reading every book they can get their hands on looking for that one answer. But it doesn't exist elsewhere, because the answer is internal.

Looking outside of yourself for answers is Not. The. Answer. You start looking for the easy button – if I could just push the button (do this one thing, take this one class, learn this one skill, the list is endless), things would be so much easier, smoother, you know, perfect. It's just not true. The only thing you need to do is stop looking externally for the answer and look inward. Start trusting yourself again.

Losing trust in yourself often happens when you start living a life of "should" instead of a life of what you truly want. Doing the work in this WELCOME Process – starting with taking ownership of your own career – is simple, but it isn't easy. Trusting that you have the answers within you takes having faith in yourself and takes trust in yourself. When you don't trust yourself, you end up overwhelmed, listening to everyone else, and unable to move forward.

Christine was my client most in this crushing, overwhelmed state. She was unable to trust her own thinking because she was so overwhelmed and kept cycling through two sets of thoughts and consequences, neither of which had any chance of ever being true. When you are overwhelmed, it is hard to see anything else. I "should" do this becomes I "have" to do this.

Not Owning Your Actions

If you don't own your actions, you will feel like you are treading water. Or you will feel like you are taking two steps forward and one step back or one step forward and two steps back. You will do all these things, take all these actions, and you will find yourself in the same struggle months or years later.

Why is that? You will do tons of things, mark tons of items off your to-do list, but it won't be any of the important things; it won't be the priority items; it won't be the most important action. You will find yourself doing the easy, mindless items on the list. You won't be doing the hard work. You won't be putting in the effort. You will be doing the easy things, not the hard, challenging ones.

Owning your actions looks like taking responsibility. Doing the adult thing. Doing the next right action, whether it is hard or not. Taking ownership – good, bad or otherwise. Not sending in your résumé until the job is closed is not taking ownership. It is waiting until the opportunity has closed and then saying, "See, I wouldn't have gotten the job anyway." It becomes a self-fulfilling prophecy of nonaction.

When I took the contracting job at Intuit after I was laid off at Sega, I didn't pursue my goal of moving to the business side. I took a job in the legal department, squarely on the legal side, not the business side. All I did was kick the can down the road. It took me another five years to learn this lesson and take ownership of my career choices to reach my goal.

Doing Other Work

Doing other work is easy. Getting distracted is easy. You may have clearly stated goals, but you are letting other things get in the way of you achieving your goals. Work often takes precedent over everything else, including family. If I don't do my job, I will be fired. The panic sets in. The action toward work stays in place. Your personal goals fall by the wayside.

In the meantime, you become overwhelmed or burned out trying to not get fired. Or at least doing the things you think you need to do to not get fired. It is like drowning. Going under slowly but not having the strength to tread water or keep your head above water.

Doing the work that you need to move forward and rise higher in your career requires you to do the important work first. Do what's important now. Do the work you have been avoiding. It is the work that requires you to know your value and share it with others. It's the work that requires you to talk about yourself and make your desires known.

One client, Nancy, kept working on her project, but she kept avoiding speaking to her boss about not being promoted in the latest rounds of promotions despite working on the most important project in the company. When she did speak to her boss, it was after he had moved on to another role in the company and it was with her current boss in the room as well. It did not have the intended effect. Avoiding the important conversation won't make it easier to have later. Have the conversation now, even if you are uncomfortable.

Not Being Honest with Yourself

It's funny how people can be honest, but not honest with themselves and their own role or responsibility in a situation. Not taking a hard, honest look at your goals and desires is the first step of self-deception. If I don't have a goal, I can just keep working at what I am doing. I can just keep going. It's much worse to have a goal and not meet it than it is to have no goal at all.

How wrong-headed is that thinking? It happens – more often than you might think. What does not being honest with yourself look like? It looks like excuses. A constant stream of excuses. I can't do that until … I can't do this until … Everything is conditional. It looks like blaming others: If he would have just done ____, then it would have all been fine. It would have worked out. It would have been perfect! Really? I call BS. It wouldn't have been perfect; you are just telling yourself that to feel better.

Being honest with yourself requires you to take an honest, hard look at what is going on. What can you control? What can you do to change the situation? What can you do to make things happen? Especially the things you want to happen. Being honest without yourself requires you to take responsibility for your role in your mess. It doesn't require you to take responsibility for others' role in the mess, just yours.

I see this obstacle most in the CEOs who want to blame everyone else for something going wrong instead of taking responsibility for their own role in the situation and for things not going well. I see this especially in hiring situations where they hire someone but don't train them properly or tell them everything they need to know to do their job and then say, "See, I knew it wouldn't work out."

Staying with a Known Mismatch

When you are in a situation with a known mismatch between what you want and what you have, it is bound to be frustrating. All the time. Supremely frustrating. This happens when you settle. You accept less than you are worth. You are staying with a known mismatch.

From a positive characterization, staying with a known mismatch looks like you are making the best of a bad situation. It may look like you took the job to make ends meet. It may look like you took a job that was a known mismatch so you could be closer to your kid's school or some other perfectly reasonable reason/excuse.

After a while, the chafing between what you want and what you have accepted or settled for begins to grate against each other and make your life unbearable. This is what happens and causes you to feel like quitting on the spot. Staying with a mismatch will just postpone the inevitable. To make a real change, you will have to choose your goals and what you want over what you have settled for.

This is what happens when you say, I'll give myself two years to find another position that is a better fit and then two years come and go without any changes. You are settling for something you know isn't right. Things won't magically get better. You must choose to make a change rather than staying in a known mismatch.

Comfort with Staying Stuck

You may have been stuck for so long that you are now feeling comfortable with being stuck. You can't even feel how off it is any longer. You may have gotten so far on your own, not seeking professional help that you don't even notice how little progress you are making.

Seeking help and taking a step forward can be scary. The feelings that it brings up can be much more overwhelming than the feeling of staying stuck. The self-loathing and the excuses don't even carry any weight any longer. They do not motivate you to take action. Of any kind. I know – I was there. I was comfortable staying stuck. It was easier than getting divorced and finding a new job at the same time. I stayed stuck until I sought the help of a coach. I had done a lot of work on myself, by myself, but I needed help to cross the finish line, and hiring a coach was just the kind of non-judgmental, unbiased help I needed. What do you need?

Hitting a wall that pushes you to the breaking point is a perfectly avoidable extreme. What if you could get the same action without having to go all the way to the wall? What if you could get help sooner?

Seeking professional help from a coach can give you a neutral perspective and help you move forward in ways you can't even imagine in the stuck place you are now.

Even if you follow every step of the WELCOME Process perfectly – any one of these obstacles can be more comfortable than the action required to make a change. Seeking help may be your best next step. I might just be the help you need to become unstuck in your career.

More Resources

Are You Ready for the Next Level? Quiz
www.sonyasigler.com/quiz

An Obstacles and Barriers to Your Success Workshop is
available on request at www.sonyasigler.com/workshops

Chapter 11:

Next Steps

Get to the Next Level

"Action is the foundational key to all success."
–Pablo Picasso

I use the WELCOME Process with clients to help them become unstuck, take action, and reach the next level of their career. Now that you've read this book, you have the same specific guidance to own and take control of your career at your fingertips. The process is deceptively simple, but you must do the work. It won't happen by itself. You've already seen the results when you leave your career in others' hands. You end up stuck, frustrated, bored, or in a dead-end position.

I read a quote by Gage Johnson, the Senior Vice President, and General Counsel at the Paramount Group, Inc., who said one of the best pieces of career advice he had ever received was: "Your job belongs to your employer. They tell you what to do, when to do it, and as long as it's not illegal, that's what you need to do, without a lot of grumbling. But you own your career. You can develop a skill set that makes you more valuable. If your employer is smart, they'll find other things for you to do. [...] People get stuck in the job and lose sight of the fact that it's not your career, It's just your job for the day." To paraphrase Gage, your job is your employer's, but your career is your own. No one else will manage your career for you.

The good news is that you have the tools you need with the WELCOME Process to manage your own career – now and in the future. If you ever become stuck again, you can refresh your career through the WELCOME Process and take action to move forward to the next level of your career.

Remember, the three secrets to reaching the next level in your career are:

Secret 1: Goals Matter

Knowing yourself, what you want, and how you want to live your life is paramount to goal setting. Having a goal will bring you clarity around what to pursue next and why.

Secret 2: Knowing Your Value Matters

With or without your consent or cultivation, your personal brand is the story told to attract people to you. Knowing what value you bring to the table, you will be able to develop stories to convey your value to others.

Secret 3: Sharing Your Value Matters

You have to get over your reluctance to be known and take personal responsibility for what others know about you. Sharing your value with others in your company and externally in your industry will make you and your work known to others rather than languishing in obscurity.

Mastering the work explained in each step of the WELCOME Process will bring you clarity around your goals, help you understand your value, and show you how to share your value and achievements with others.

The WELCOME to the Next Level Process is here to help you become unstuck, take action, and rise higher in your career at any time. The steps of the WELCOME Process are:

Step 1: Who Are You?
Take a look at your fundamental beliefs and values and really peel back the layers of your beliefs to identify what is most important to you.

Step 2: Envision Your Work-Life Mix
Look at your entire life picture – the mix of what you want at work and what you want in your home life, as the two are inextricably intertwined.

Step 3: Locate the Gaps
The gap between what you want and what you have will give you guidance on what to change and what to do next. The bigger the gap, the more frustrated and stuck you are. The smaller the gap, the happier and more satisfied you will be with your career.

Step 4: Call Out Your Strengths
Define your strengths and skills to make it easier to articulate these to others.

Step 5: <u>O</u>wn Your Value

Developing authentic and memorable stories that explain or showcase your experience makes it easier for you to share your value with others. Owning your achievements and stories gives you the confidence to share these stories with others.

Step 6: <u>M</u>ake Yourself Known Internally

Being known by others is the key to getting promoted and any job, especially your next job. Sharing your work and your stories internally at your own company will make your work more widely known.

Step 7: <u>E</u>xternally Become Known

Sharing your work and stories externally beyond your company, throughout your industry, and beyond will get you noticed in a broader network. Should you decide to leave your job, you will have already cultivated a network to help you move to the next level.

I don't want you to spend one more day than you have to in a job where you are stuck or in a job you hate. I want you to understand your worth and achieve your potential. I want you to reach the next level!

Or if you are in a mind-set where you have accepted that you can't get promoted in your current job, I want you to find a job elsewhere that takes you to the next level of your career.

Your next steps are to take control of your career back into your own hands and chart your own course. Doing the work in each step of the WELCOME Process will take thought and reflection. But I know you can do it, because you want to make a change. You are ready to make a change; otherwise, you wouldn't have read this book!

Acknowledgements

This book has been on my mind for many years, or rather a book has been on my mind since I started working as an attorney. I wanted a book of stories written by women in the workplace who had already been where I am – I wanted to call it "If I Knew Then What I Know Now." I wanted to learn from their mistakes, from their experience. I wanted a leg up. I didn't want there to be a glass ceiling, Even though this book is a little different from the book I had imagined all those years ago, I still wish I had *this* book in my hands during my first job when I realized that there was no career path and that I would have to make my own.

I've encountered many people along the way who have helped make this book possible. My first mentor, my mother, Lee Sigler, has been there every step of the way – encouraging me, supporting me. I can't thank her enough for being an amazing role model and for quietly believing in me even when I didn't believe in myself. She started me on my writing career with a Ziggy diary when I was about ten. I've come a long way in my writing life since then – thank you, Mom!

I'd like to thank my brother, who would not so subtly ask me every time he was in town – "So, how's your book going? When is it going to be out?" We'd inevitably have long, wine-filled conversations and talk about our careers and the unexpected twists and turns they had taken. He specifically encouraged me to write three separate books rather than one large *Moby-Dick* wannabe book. When I began my coaching business, he also told me I didn't charge enough for my services. Thank you, Shane, for those two very useful pieces of advice!

You never know where your writing inspiration will come from – mine came from a pacing-partner-like relationship with my best friend from college, Graciela Tiscareno-Sato. She, with my encouragement, published a chapter in an anthology about an episode from our Cal Band days, which launched her writing career. She in turn encouraged me to publish a story about another episode from our college days – as that story is not fit for public consumption, I definitely did not contribute a story to that Cal anthology. She was there by my side in January 2015 as we co-presented the topic of this book as part of a talk on the Top 10 Tips to Manage Your Career. She's been with me every step of the way, even as I coached her through being overwhelmed with her own company and personal life. Thank you for being my champion throughout our lives and my mentor throughout this book publishing process.

My Vistage Group and their contribution to making this book a reality has been invaluable. Lance Descourouez, our chair, has been a fearless supporter since I joined his group in 2012. He tries to soften all my hard edges while encouraging me to be me and do what I do best – see others for who they are. Debbie Simoni – you have allowed me to coach you and inspire you all these years so that you can see how amazing you are. Pam Isom, wow, where do I start? If I could have a smidgen of your discipline and your drive, what else could I do and accomplish. You, as a business owner and a mom of two amazing daughters, are an inspiration to me as I launch my own business and raise my three sons! Tony Lopez, you have challenged me to be better, do better, and to finish this darn book before you! More importantly, you have started me and my husband and three boys down a path to financial independence, for which I cannot thank you enough. Nader Vasseghi, watching you write your book your own way, make your own cover, and market it in your own quiet way has inspired me to be a more involved artist and author. Katey Dallosto, whether you know it or not, you lit a fire under me to publish this book and to talk about what I do with more people than my immediate contacts. Nirmal Chandrasekaran, thank you for inspiring me to be a better, more patient coach. Rob Christopher, you have inspired me through your own book-writing process to finally get this book out of my head and on to the paper, no matter what it took! To the remaining members of TA1123 group – thank you all for your continued support and encouragement.

I want to thank all of my consulting and coaching clients for the past twenty years. Thank you for allowing me the privilege of coaching you and learning from you. I can't begin to name all of you individually, but you know who you are and I especially want to make sure that you know how much I appreciate you and applaud you for the work you have done and for levels you have reached in your careers. Congratulations – your ownership of your own career and your hard work has paid off!

Thank you to the attendees of the inaugural class of Unstuck: Getting to the Next Level. You have come along for a wild ride – being the first to go through the whole set of classes at once, being willing to take a leap of faith while this book was still in development, and being willing to do the work and take your own career and life to the next level. Bravo! And thank you to each of you: Yulia Azriel, Frank Bravo, Tanya Chase, Heather Crowell, Cheryl Frank Dutton, Bernice Gonzales, Daya Jaggers, Marjorie Kline, Deborah Mannia, Cherie Morgan, Diane Rutledge, Elysia Skye, Stephen Smith, Vivien Ting, and Amy Walsh.

Thank you to Denise Brosseau, my foreword author, for your constant and continued support. It's been an absolute pleasure to know and work with you all these years. The Author Incubator and the brains behind it, Angela Lauria, have given me the final push I needed to get this book into your hands. Thank you as well to David Hancock and the Morgan James Publishing team for helping me bring this book to print.

Thank you to Ellen Bradley for encouraging me to write higher. Thank you to Emily Wanderer Cohen for showing me how it is done! Reconnecting with you and seeing your success has provided me with a wonderful role model to make a difference.

My awesome, supportive book launch team – thank you for hopping on board with me and helping launch this book! It was indeed a team effort, and I couldn't have done this without you! Thank you: Cynthia Alberth, Velia Anderson, Connie Barton Barba, Bobbi Basile, Patti Bouchard, Ellen Jennings Bradley, Frank Bravo, Winslow Chapman, Tanya Chase, Emily Wanderer Cohen, Heather Crowell, Susan Fenimore Dworak, Gill Curry, Katey Dallosto, Heather DeVore, Cheryl Frank Dutton, Lauren Ganem, Edmund Goh, Julia Goldstein, Bernice Gonzalez, Patricia Hawkes, Pam Heffley, Amy Henley, Joyce Irby, Julie

Lanesey, Robert LoBue, Tony Lopez, Deborah Mannia, Diane Ehn Martin, Ken Mayer, Terri Umphress McDowell, Nicole Reihl Molloy, Cherie Morgan, Diane Morgan, Houston Morgan, Juli-anne Davis Morgan, Deborah Moritz-Farr, Ron Peppe, Claire Phillips, Fay Rector, Robbie Reed-Moffat, Linsey Richmond, Cassandra Roy, Diane Rutledge, Michelle Sandusky, Adam Sigler, Ginger Silverman, Elysia Skye, Leslie Svanevik, Carol Torno, Lee Torno, Ana Carolina Uribe, Amy Walsh, Tom Wills, Susan Zaro.

I'd like to acknowledge you, the reader, for having the courage to pick up this book and do the work to make yourself known for who you are. Taking charge of your own career is a big step and I love that you are willing to be authentic and share your value with the world.

Finally, I would like to thank my most ardent supporter: my husband, Keir Morgan. His encouragement has been unwavering from almost the moment I met him. He said to me early in our dating life – "If you've been this successful so far without unconditional support, just think how much more successful you will be when you have someone supportive by your side." Yes, indeed. My husband encouraged me to start my own consulting/coaching company to help as many people as possible transform their lives into exactly what they want. Thank you, my love, for all of your support in making my company and this book a reality.

Thank You

Thank you so much for reading this book. The fact that you've reached this point tells me that you are ready to make a change. You are ready to become unstuck and own your career. You are ready to do the important work to reach the next level of your career.

To support you in moving forward, I created the **Are You Ready for the Next Level? Quiz**. It is a simple diagnostic assessment to help you get crystal-clear about whether you are ready to make a move – to change roles, to take on a new project, to get promoted, or to move to another company.

You can take this free **Are You Ready for the Next Level? Quiz** on my website at http://www.sonyasigler.com/quiz

I'd love to hear from you and hear about your successes. You can share your stories, vision boards, and successes with me through email at info@sonyasigler.com.

Finally – if you find a typo or editing issue, please drop me a note at info@sonyasigler.com and let me know so I can fix it. I hate reading errors in other's books, and I don't want them in mine! If you alert me to a typo I don't know about yet, as a thank you, I'll give you (and your work) a shout out in my social media world. Let me know two things: (1) what the typo is and (2) something about you that you want me to share with others to help you move forward in your own career.

I look forward to hearing more about you reaching YOUR next level.

About the Author

Sonya L. Sigler is the founder of PractiGal LLC and is the creator of the WELCOME to the Next Level Process. She created this WELCOME Process to effectively sell herself when she needed to figure out a clear path forward professionally and personally. Having learned to do this work the hard way, Sonya now builds powerful storytellers who can

then refine and polish their personal brand. This work empowers others to align their work and life visions and to approach both with a renewed vigor.

For the last twenty years, Sonya has worked with founders, team leaders, and their employees one-on-one and as teams to create real-world game plans for their company and products that are realistic, practical, and achievable. The end result of this work is building effective, collaborative teams and happy, satisfied employees who then work together to take the business to the next level.

Sonya started her career as an in-house lawyer with Sega and discovered that she likes to build new processes and systems and mentor others. As a mentor, one of the most frequently asked questions Sonya hears is *Can you help me figure out what to do next?* Through helping other answer that question, and more, Sonya became a leadership success coach. She has helped hundreds of highly motivated professional women (and enlightened and progressive men) be known for who they are and take ownership of their own career to reach the next level.

Sonya lives in the San Francisco Bay Area, with her husband and two cats and occasionally her three sons when they are home from college. Most of the time, she can be found volunteering in her community, performing on stage, raising money, or traveling the world to explore different cultures, cuisines, and meet new people.

About PractiGal LLC

Sonya Sigler founded PractiGal to help entrepreneurs, lawyers, and leaders breakthrough barriers and reframe their goals to take action. The PractiGal mission is to build powerful storytellers and help them be known for who they are and take control of their own business or career path. PractiGal works with companies to build effective, collaborative teams which not only necessitates the work at a team or company level but at the individual level as well. When individuals take ownership of their career, goals, role, and attitude, they become more effective and collaborative team members. All of this results in happy, satisfied employees working on effective and productive teams.

Contact Info:

Email: Info@sonyasigler.com

Website: www.sonyasigler.com

LinkedIn: www.linkedin.com/in/sonyasigler

CPSIA information can be obtained
at www.ICGtesting.com
Printed in the USA
JSHW020048020720
6423JS00001B/51